Your Enemies Waiting for you to find them

Nothing is written in Stone

Bonnie Baumgartner

Copyright © 2009 Bonnie Baumgartner
All rights reserved.

ISBN: 1-4392-4116-3
ISBN-13: 9781439241165

To order additional copies, please contact us.
BookSurge
www.booksurge.com
1-866-308-6235
orders@booksurge.com

Table of Contents for

Your ENTOURAGE is WAITING for you to find them
NOTHING is written in STONE
Book 22

Introduction vii
Acknowledgments xv
About Me. xix

Chapter 1 **MULTIDIMENSION to LINEAR and Back** 1
Our CELLS REMEMBER. 7
STUCK POINTS. 16

Chapter 2 **ENTOURAGE THERAPY** RUTH . . 27

Chapter 3 **Svali Speaks** on Programming. 69
WOLF, BEAR, CROW programming 130

Chapter 4 **COSMIC FLOW**. **135**

Chapter 5 **3rd, 4th and 5th DIMENSION** . . **167**
SUN or PORTAL. 181

Chapter 6 **Photons** 197
VIKINGS 205
SOME NUMEROLOGY 210

My Book list. 231

my website is www.**mysticknowing.com**
And NOW an on line **dictionary** for you.

Introduction

Your ENTOURAGE is WAITING for you to find them
NOTHING is written in STONE
Book 22

With the advent of the veil came the ILLUSION of separation from our entourage. "The veil", isn't a place or thing it's a dynamic energy that surrounds our very consciousness and every cell of the biology. The veil is BETWEEN you and your invisible aspects between the 3rd dimensional illusion and multiple dimensions and reality. The qualities the veil has kept hidden has been from the human not from our 90%er.
All is in change and evolution NOW. The purpose of earth and the surrounding celestial bodies is to UNFOLD and EVOLVE your life, balancing and working with

your soul and the invisible realm. This requires your CONSCIOUS positive THOUGHT first followed with the soul's input and synchronicities and then YOUR responsible action. We take **responsibility** for sustaining ourself by nurturing OUR joy and well-being. Joy in life requires **ATTENTION** and **focus**.

Always be aware that we are eternally moving and evolving whether we pay attention or not. Life is the experience, and discovery of THE SELF. When your focus is scattered you cannot maintain harmony and balance. *The purpose of the joyful life* is to maintain harmony and balance while expanding.

When you can fully stay in present time you can acsess the three aspects of linear time, past, present and future or the timelessness of multidimensions. The days of Lemuria and Atlantis are back for us to alter the outcome.

The reason cults and our government start their programming on fetuses and infants is because what is done to the **innocent trusting child** has a 100 times the impact than it would to the adult.

Combine childhood traumas, church, government, school, work and our "DNA set up at birth" and you know why so many humans are just NUMB **robots**. Awareness of how you have been SHAPED gives you the power to move beyond that programming developed to control you. DNA is crystalline and a perfect reciever, electromagnetic transmitter and amplifier. Each cell in our biology is a liquid crystal. Our cells are structured and function like a silicon chip. Cells function as the hard drive and the DNA holds the genetic memory. The more powerful the information is the greater the potential is for creation or destruction.

The body and brain are receivers and transmitters of information not unlike a computer. We take electromagnetic waves converting them into feelings and thoughts. We create our reality based on the consciousness we posses and what we intend to create for ourself in this ILLUSION of DISCONNECTION we keep returning to until we see that it IS an ILLUSION and we move out of the prison with NO BARS we are in. The reptilians made earth a prison and slave camp for humans. The reptilians had advanced knowledge technowledgy, in math, astronomy and cosmic cycles, which they keept secret and passed on through a select few reptillians and some hybreds of reptilian and human. The reptilian bloodline hybreds took over and ran the ancient mystery schools-they manipulated themselves into positions of power covertly called the illumanati, Satanism, Jesuits, Knights Templar, Freemason's and on and on.

We live in multiple energy fields that our brain DOES NOT decode because the brain is not programmed to see them. **We decode REALITY to fit the beliefs FORCED on us with all the programming.** ANY ridged belief LIMITS your ability to see a larger picture than we have been trained to see.

FIXED OPINIONS create a dense vortex in the neuron network and ridged beliefs reinforce each other. When two or more humans have ridged beliefs they think apose each other you can play one against the other to divide and conqure the human or humans. What we believe we create.

ENTOURAGE UPDATE

Your entourage is made up of aspects of YOU. Most of our parts are invisible. Those aspects have different vibrations of awareness and some are dark or light and many shades of gray. Historically we felt we could send the dark gray and black off someplace or wall it off in some way.
That is not the way the universe works.
That is why the human MUST DISCERN what is coming from their light bits and what is coming from their dark bits. Because we are functioning in a free will zone. We are responsible for all our aspects, the dark, gray and light with all their various vibrations of awareness. You need to be aware of the aspect within your entourage answering you questions and what vibration

of awareness they are coming from if you care to evolve spiritually. The human is to DECIDE which aspect or vibration they want to follow the dark, gray or light suggestions.

NOT deciding means you will be controlled or guided by the strongest aspect of you. It is your choice. You can CHOOSE to give your power away. When you want to make LIGHT choices each day you will need to be very alert at first until you get the hang of it. The human is also RESPONSIBLE for educating their dark aspects and bring them to the light way of reasoning and viewing choices.

When talking to your entourage and asking for guidance and they suggest you DO rescue another, ASK is this coming from the DARK bits of me?

They will say YES if that is true.

You need to pick your direction.

KNOW you are not the victim of any outside source or energy; you carry the darkness within you to understand contrast. When you ask your entourage a question and suspect the dark bits are supplying the answers. Some of us avoid or deny this much honesty and will say, "I can't hear." Generally that is a YES or your question is too broad for them to answer.

Ask just one question at a time so the answers are clear to you. A WORLD OF PEACE and HARMONY IS NOT A POSSIBILITY WITHOUT COMPASSION. Reptilians have NO compassion, which is why they cannot exist in higher vibrations.

Acknowledgments

I am greatful to the **COUNCIL of TEACHERS** that is made up of human and angelic educators offering to be an example and helping others when asked. They have studied the SPIRITUAL aspects of moving to higher levels of compassion on both sides of the veil. The council of teachers evaluate unexplored physical and none physical dimensions or different places of awareness and the way they function.
Teachers are TEMPLATE makers. **We LEARN by teaching and we teach by LISTENING.**

I want to thank and am very grateful to all those with biology and WITHOUT biology that have trusted me to work with them. I am very grateful to the invisible realm that tirelessly continues to work hard to get the humans through their ascension process THANK YOU.

Kryon of Magnetic Service, channeled by **Lee Carroll** kryon.com

The Group channeled by **Steve Rother** Lightworker.com

David Icke http://www.david-icke.com

I am grateful for the HUMANS that have helped me with their consciousness, creativity and time.

Kelly Arbogast who brainstorms with me and shares his vast knowledge. He created and serves as the Webmaster on the Mystic Knowing website. http://www.mysticknowing.com

Dan Laudicina who gives a different point of perception and fills in awareness that I miss.

He helped fill out information I lacked.

Becky Beebe who sees pictures and stories to add different levels of consciousness to our thoughts and ideas.

Torben Hansen, who feels, knows and shares his higher mental fields and personal knowledge. Torben facilitates other humans going through their awakening process. Torben is sensitive to the patterns we get "stuck in," and helps people to evolve out of the repetitive behaviors we use to distract ourselves with.
http://www.look4insight.com
http://awarenesshealsme.com

About Me

I have been an educational therapist for the past sixteen years and have done private therapy with children, adults and families. I understand how devastating CHILD abuse is and how it will negatively affect a person of any age. For the past 40 years, I have taught emotionally challenged and severely learning disabled students and adults from grades 3-12 in public schools as well as in my own private school, these experiences have showed me what works and what does not work.

Your entourage has the entire story along with everyone else's story and is happy to share it WHEN you are ready to hear it **JUST ASK** them. **Your ENTOURAGE is WAITING for you to find them.**

The FULL knowledge of what actually happened to you and your reaction to what happened will heal your addictions and self-destructive patterns you hold dear. PUTTING a pretty story on your childhood experiences will NOT CHANGE ANYTHING and it never has. Clinging to a pretty story will slow or stop your healing and ascension.

The "cause and effect" of things have always fascinated me and I always want to "know more" so I studied the field of psychology and sociology my entire existence and many more than this life time.

Inside you KNOW
Bonnie

Chapter 1
MULTIDIMENSION to LINEAR and Back

In the beginning we were an integral part of the creator and "All That Is" there was no SEPARATION. The legion of light is able to do **all things** with the exception of one. It could not **study it self** because there was no CONTRAST or duality. When left HOME we were imprinted with duality in our DNA so our reality was that of opposites. We ONLY saw light when darkness was present. We only saw love when FEAR was known. IN this illusion we saw opposite ends of our *feelings and emotions and felt all those in between.* When we were traumatized too much we shut down our FEELING and abandoned our biology.

We can only grow spiritually and ascend by **getting BACK INTO our BIOLOGY stay there and FEEL everything.** Our biology helped us with contrasts and creating more matter. IF we are pretty or ugly, fat or thin, old or young, sick or well. Our biology is **MATTER and from the earth** and enables us to experience contrast Biology is born of the earth and returns to the earth. The biology is a VRHICLE for the higher self or soul to have experiences in. Our BIOLOGY is NOT galactic or a spiritual body.

The human lessons in duality have been completed for many. With the frequencies of duality we learned a lot about greed, fear and scarcity. Now we are moving from duality to TRIALITY. The higher self bends the straight line of duality into a triangle. The new connection to the higher self or your entourage still has duality BUT the higher self, BALANCES duality into a CIRCLE and a lot of areas of **separation** are ending. The separation of countries needs to end also. All OUR careful separations to define our self clearly are coming back together as one. Everyone will be part of each other AGAIN.

We are teaching our self now and THE JOURNEY IS the school or classroom. When we **feel connected** to everything we are filled with love and compassion. This can only happen after you get back in your biology and you locate and communicate with your entourage so you can AWAKEN. You need to stop BLAMING, **controlling**, *forcing* and JUDGING. You need to control your **thoughts** and released the guilt, worry, compromise and doubt.

The purpose of earth and the surrounding celestial bodies is to CHANGE and EVOLVE YOUR life. Take **responsibility for these changes** by nurturing YOUR joy and YOUR wellbeing. We are shifting our awareness from the finite to INFINITE. Form the past and future and to all the dimensions while remaining in PRESENT TIME. We create each moment in concert with our entourage. Always be aware that we are eternally *moving and evolving* whether you are paying attention or not. Life is the discovery of THE SELF through experiences. The legion of light is getting to know and see itself with the help of our vehicle or biology.

JOY of life or experiences requires your ATTENTION and **focus**. When your focus is SCATTERED, you cannot maintain harmony and balance. *The purpose of life* is to maintain harmony and balance while JOYFULLY expanding while in the flow.

When you can fully stay in present time you can access the three aspects of LINEAR time, past, present and future or the timelessness of multidimensions is also available. Humans are biologies with souls in them that have **amnesia** UNTIL they awaken. Until you are CONSCIOUS you are living a life with RULES you HAVE been unaware of the universal laws or the rules of compassion and love or the VERY complex science of light.

Feelings of unworthiness and not loving the self will prevent you from following "the laws and levels of compassion" and love the earth was formed with. Even our FAMILIES, countries and planets are subject to the laws of COMPASSION love and the universe.

Access into the crystalline vibration is denied to those that blame, deny, doubt, compromise or judge themselves along with those stuck in the victim predator and witness band of low vibration. As long as you believe you are flawed **"so it is."** YOU have triggered the "law of attraction" and

Your Entourage is Waiting for you to find them

continue to pull in more of what you already have. Your **vibrational pattern** holds you in your CHOSEN vibration. The laws of LOVE do not care if your choice is conscious or unconscious. What you feel passionately about **YOU created more of** especially when it is hate or fear or abuse or depression.

To release YOUR passionate negative creation, CHANGE YOUR THOUGHTS. Change your thoughts to change your vibration. Yes it is all an act of YOUR WILL until you create a joyful experience for yourself. When most humans in a group have the same vibration, OR when a *STRONG minority EXPRESSES on the groups behalf,* it becomes GROUP WILL. In both individual thought or group thought or planetary thought or galactic thought along with ALL your minute-by-minute actions you create a vibration.

Two families living next to each other can have totally different vibrations. When they interact with each other a lot the law of entrainment gets triggered. The law of entrainment says THAT two resonance's existing in the same location **MUST adjust**

and combine generally in a middle range UNLESS one is very strongly pulling to their vibration.

We can change and grow as we learn to take back our power, **set boundaries** and RECLAIM our love of self there is a profound effect on us and in our relationships. The romantic relationships, has been the most difficult. Historically, relationships were based on DEPENDENCE, **security** and a desire to find VALIDATION of the self from people and things outside of us. We agreed to share the load, and reap the rewards.

Humans are a stream of motion in the now moment of AWARENESS or unconsciousness. Individual CONSCIOUS or UNCONSCIOUSNESS is subjected to the particular group of vibrations or flow of awareness. There is "the NOW we are aware of" and a greater NOW we are not so aware of. Trying to know more about a greater NOW we are not so aware of is the challenge. Responding creatively to each and every challenge we face allows for many possibilities we never even considered. Embracing our experiences allows for continuous RECONFIGURATION of the reality we experience. A creative respond to our ever-changing moments are dependent on our ability to respond and embrace the RANDONESS of our experiences. Things that are difficult DO not mean things have gone wrong.

Our CELLS REMEMBER

Cellular memory or energy stamps operate on a planetary basis ALSO. Cellular memory is playing a major role in some of the conflicts, tragedies and upheavals on earth. Resolution of cellular memory and its role in cosmic justice, karma or memory is playing out now. Many humans on earth have brought their energy stamps with them from parts of this galaxy and many lifetimes on other planets.

Humans of earth are allowing entities from other parts of this galaxy to have an opportunity to release the intense emotional energy stamp of the destruction of their plant similar to the experiences we had at the end of Atlantis when our greed and desire for control of others unbalanced our energy too far to get back in balance.

Individuals, families, groups, the earth and other planets despite their BEST intentions may well repeat a pattern that is self destructive and can end in their destruction. Alice Miller calls this the compulsion to repeat. We compulsively repeated a behavior pattern to understand what happened in our past so we can heal that trauma and resulting behavior our **AWARENESS heals us or me**. We each need to SEE and own the TRUTH of our experiences. When you are unwilling to see and own your reality you WILL REPEATE and repeate the pattern UNTIL you do see and own the truth of your experiences.

There is a cellular memory of these patterns in our DNA that follow us lifetime after lifetime until we gather the wisdom. The lifetime we are in now was dictated by the events of our previous life. The energies of your current lifetime will bring you into situations that are in resonance with your cellular memories.

What you think, feel and believe is important, for your vibrations of intention either add to the problems of earth and humanity or add to the collective thought form of hope, inspiration and victory over the pain, suffering and chaos of the third and fourth-dimensional world.

20% of the current human population centered mostly in the Middle East is ANUNNAKI. They are on earth at this time to re-experience the trauma of their destruction and hopefully gain the WISDOM and change their outcome this time around they are reptilian.

Anunnaki or Gray's or Orion entities from the star system we call Sirius have brought their cellular memories of earlier conflicts on stars distant from us. They are playing the darkest of the dark energy of SEPARATION. They existed for centuries and millennia before we appeared on earth. These star systems went through many advanced stages of technology and spirituality with some catastrophic events. The energies and conflicts from their earlier star systems in some cases led to the severe destructions of a planetary system and they brought their energy stamps or cell memories with them. They are looking to heal those self-destructive patters of behavior with AWARENESS. With the awareness of what REALLY happened they can gain the wisdom and embrace their darkness and raise their vibration a notch. The Earth currently has similar energies like those earlier planetary civilizations had with their greed and desire to control others.

Humans have agreed to assist Anunnaki on their journey back to the legion of light. Anunnaki with a low vibration cannot access information as humans can when we open UP to love, light and compassion. They only have **low-level survival truths.** Kill or be killed. Those of low vibration levels have rather restricted LEVELS OF INFORMATION and awareness. They are not in touch with their pain and trauma.

The Anunnaki are walking a fine line. They push agendas that will prevent reconnection with the earth energetically. They use fear and a **FALSE sense of action**. They want expansion of nuclear programs and Armageddon and fear to feed from. In the third dimension this is not healthy or in harmony with the earth and crystalline energy. They have not learned to live in balance with a celestial body. As our vibration rises they may need to move to another planet to discharge their cell memories. As of 1987 humans have the OPTION to completely release karma and change their astrological imprint. The things that imprint your personality with YOUR characteristics that shape you.

It is **NOT appropriate** to sacrifice YOU, your dreams and wishes for another. It is **NOT appropriate** for those in your life to make sacrifices or enable you to be DEPENDENT on them. Make loving yourself YOUR greatest priority. After eons of time, self-love and self-realization have become labeled as selfish behavior in an effort to control you. Out of that control is born the saying "THINK of the FAMILY" forget about YOU and do what is best for the family the church your job. Who is happy or joyful in that situation? No one is loving them self or creating a higher vibration.

Sacrifice is NOT LOVE, sacrifice is control and misery loving company. Through so many centuries of JUDGEMENT, **fear,** ANGER and **control** loving yourself has become something strange. The legion of light experiences through and with all entities and grows from those experiences. All

KNOWING is **not** knowing all the FACTS and collected knowledge. It is about you and your experiences and about your collected EMOTIONS and your access to those emotions and feelings so we are better able to manage our FEELINGS and thoughts. From our emotional experiences we gather our spiritual WISDOM.

Our negative emotions are the **energetic glue** that holds our pockets of dense matter in our aura. Releasing negative emotions and wounds tied to people and events allow you to move forward in present time with all of your pieces and parts fully present. Ask your entourage or soul to help.

Emotions are the FUEL that **propels our behavior** and MORALITY. We create the way WE FEEL EMOTIONALLY for good or bad. EMOTIONS with their dramas belong to the LITTLE human and are **easily manipulated or controlled** by others when you are NOT **in LOVE with YOURSELF.** Our emotions and thoughts can easily go off into misdirected energy preventing spiritual awareness and wisdom to be SEEN. When you are ready to move into oneness you accept and embrace ALL of your emotions. Think of your emotions as your PARTNER in awareness, your invisible parts SPEAKING to you through your emotions. You are or need to be in total compassion for YOURSELF first. The more you partner with your emotions as the loving **instructor and friend** they are, the more you value your human self. The more self-love you have, the more you are brought back to your perfection.

JUDGMENT

Judgment is a human thought form. A thought form is *a temporary living entity* of *intense activity* animated by the idea that generated it. A thought form may be benevolent or malevolent. JUDGMENT does not really exist on higher vibrational planes, but it is understood. Judgment exists and operates within duality. In higher vibrations FOR EXAMPLE as soon as you think a thought such as "I should have been forgiving" you instantly ***BECOME* more *forgiving***. YOU change, "I should have" into I DID forgive. Your expanded self allows you to explore the concept of judgment, but will not allow you to dwell on the concept. On the other side of the veil you have moved a bit beyond duality. You can move even farther away from duality by directing your thoughts elsewhere.

As you think, YOU ARE.

Higher dimensional races have communicated with us all along using the language of light but we did not recognize it for what it was. There will be many new ways given to us to learn the language. Instead of communicating with just words or gestures we can use GUT level or FEELING communication with few or no words. We can communicate on a soul-to-soul level to create new depth in communication with others. Go right to the soul level of another, which is ALSO YOU and the part you share with them, you can KNOW their feelings.

We crave unity and not extreme separation. We never loose our sacred space or our heritage even though we might forget about it. We are finding new connections and as that takes place humans will unite releasing the need for separation of hearts.

All entities or consciousness will speak to you when you LISTEN. See and read from a higher point of perception. As we evolve our belief systems need to stay flexible. Rigid beliefs support separation. Allow your brain, mind and heart to open to NEW possibilities never seen before. MIND is the energy of the physical brain. Our mind is a dynamic receiver, processor and transmitter available for your exclusive use to work with your resonance. You cannot fail and are never alone. Everything spiritual is solution oriented. Multidimensional **fifth dimensional** minds are more harmonic and greater than linear minds.

The pathways taken by younger minds will be different than those that have already been explored. The question posed will be looked at in a variety of different ways yielding many different results. You can do nothing wrong. Your soul guides and directs all. Even the most evil people have a place to play because this truth is an illusion except for the Oneness that is expressed through love and joy.

There is no staying the same NOT EVER. The universe is in constant expansion and movement. And as you learn to FLOW with that constant movement, your life becomes easier and more enjoyable. Release control and needing someone else to be something they are not. Let go of your own need to be perfect and have it done your way. Appreciate the thoughts of another entity there is no need to agree with them.

When we present our entourage with questions, concerns or issues it is to increase our **clarity** or LIGHT. Please be as present as you possibly can if you want to communicate. Healing and guidance can be the same thing. Channeled guidance can relieve and release conflicts within you that block the flow of your wisdom. Practice the guidance you get when you get it or the guidance fades and diminishes. Blame will not get you desirable results. Speak softly and you will hear more. Know that logic and reason can hide wisdom.

STUCK POINTS

Most humans that have got STUCK on their spiritual path and reverted to letting their little human run them generally have a childhood issue or many issues to address. When the little human gets greedy, proud, money hungry and wants to control others they are doing what was done to them by a person with a fair amount of darkness. They are NOT in love with themselves and are trying to COMPENSATE for their LOW self-esteem or feelings of worthlessness they picked up during their childhood.

The trusting innocent child is a **hundred times more sensitive** to what happens to them than the average adult is. The child generally reads other's thoughts taking them VERY seriously especially when they are dark. CHILDREN *are angels in disguise.* LITERALLY they are mature angels even if they are in little human biology. With ALL of US on earth being MATURE ANGELS we can all develop freely the way we want to develop and create.

The parent NEVER ever OWNS the child. They are disguised as your children but they are souled mature beings. The parent only ACCEPTS THE **RESPONSIBILITY** of bringing the child into the world and for a SHORT time cares for the child and then grants them their freedom at the age of 18 years in America. A parent is to give them food, shelter and help educate them in the early stages of life and then LET GO of that responsibility. Children are NOT your life long personal friends to jerk around forever either. Children are not around to CARRY your darkness. Own your issues and stop passing them on to your children and others. The time to take responsibility for you and all your thoughts and beliefs is NOW.

The ADULT thoughts and behaviors ARE the result of their childhood experiences. The ADULT has learned to value and love them self based on childhood lessons. When the one that cared for the child is darker than light the picture is not so pretty.

The human stuck and unable to move forward on their spiritual path is also having trouble loving themselves because of childhood experiences they prettified or minimized or failed to see the big picture. The way to clear up childhood things keeping you stuck is to ask for help and clarification from your entourage.

Dissociative Identity Disorder (DID) or the old term Multiple personality Disorder (MPD) is the result of **severe childhood trauma**, usually sexual and physical abuse. It is a coping mechanism in young children.

Your Entourage is Waiting for you to find them

They develop other personalities to deal with the intense pain, fear, and danger they experienced as a child. As the child grows older this dissociation ceases to be a coping mechanism and becomes a STUCK point to normal growth and functioning in their life.

Human's, are a conglomerate of parts that are visible and invisible. In the soup of energy that IS your entourage THERE WILL be some DARK energy MIXED with your light energy and we are working to bring our dark parts into the light. That is why it is so important for the **human to DISCERN** what is coming from their light bits and what is coming from their dark bits as we are functioning in a free will zone they are all present so your discernment will be in constant use.

You are not the victim of any outside source or energy you carry the darkness and light within you to understand contrast better and master discernment. When you ask your entourage a question and suspect the dark bits are supplying the answer. ASK is this answer from my dark bits? They will say "yes." Then show love and compassion for the dark so it can know and feel the love, compassion and light. The dark bits do not realize they can move into the light and you can guide them.

Many humans have created a childhood story that does not match the facts of what really happened to them. They created a childhood for themselves that they could live with. Generally humans have PRETTIFIED their story AND denied the facts. The EMOTIONAL traumas or love BONDS have not been acknowledged and accepted and will not release until the truth is honored, embraced and melded with.

We heal and move on when the childhood issues giving us grief are owned and melded. Depending on your vibration level your entourage might give a third dimensional slide show or possibly a feeling event and awareness. Your entourage can give you the facts and feelings or a "slide show" or a "show of FEELINGS and EMOTIONS". All you need do is ask and feel. Over the period of days they will give a feeling and you might get a memory or six. Then another feeling and memory and this will go on until you have a good feel for what REALLY happened during your childhood.

Most of us feel we have come to terms with our childhood experiences. We FEEL that we have worked on and released our childhood drama and TRAUMA. We feel it is ancient history and we need to get OVER it. Our parents LOVED us! They said that so it is true.

Let me remind you that most of our parents had rather dark energy and were probably not very truthful. At birth we come in with the dark and light balance the planet had that day and before 1987 it was always darker than light. Frequently people have children to make them suffer just as they did when they were a child. The adult says "I love my child" but frequently that means I love to torment my child just as I was tormented. "I do not want my child to be happier than I am" so I control them as I was controlled.

ANOTHER CONSIDERATION

In the higher vibrating crystalline energy there are many more layers and VERY detailed aspects we need to have in our awareness to ascend. You need to FEEL the abandonment, pain, betrayed, fear and/or isolation you experienced. You need to know your father and you had a special bond no one else in the family had. You need to FEEL what it was like to be offered up to another family member or a stranger by your mom because she was unable to LOVE herself and consequently was unable to be loving toward you or care how much you suffered. She always suffers more than you do, ask her if you don't believe me, she'll tell you all about it.

Do not excuse or protect the adult that wounded you because that is a way to AVOID feeling exactly what you the child FELT. You must reexperience YOUR real FEELINGS.

An example of the detail the invisible realm is going into: Jan knew she had been forced as a four-year-old child and older to give oral sex to her father and other adult men. She had worked with a therapist to heal that trauma. In her fifties she had some dental work done which restimulated that on going trauma. Her entourage wanted other layers of that abuse addressed!

1. After the dental work she could not relax her jaws. Her entourage and biology wanted her to remember how painful that was for a small-mouthed child to do for an adult male penis.

2. Jan blamed her mouth for upsetting the men when her teeth touched a penis. She needed to discern it was the men at fault and NOT her small mouth. Her small mouth and teeth needed gratitude for their service to her.

3. There are times Jan stuffs food in her mouth. If she is to be forced to have things stuffed in her mouth SHE wants to have the control over what gets stuffed in.

4. Jan always keeps something in her mouth that tastes good as an adult, like gum or candy. Those men were so nasty tasting and scary.

5. A four year old has a small mouth compared to many adult penises so they dislocated her jaw which has been a re-occurring issue throughout her life and the dentist did it once again.

6. The above experiences had happened in many lifetimes.

7. Her pain from the dental work and extractions was great because there was "20% PRESENT time pain" along with the "80% past time pain of the childhood abuse." Jan was not able to honor and embrace HER pain during her childhood; it needed to be done as an adult.

All conflicts, UNRESOLVED issues or injustices that **YOU have experienced** or THOUGHT you experienced in this and other lifetimes or EVEN between lifetimes need **resolution now** before you can meld completely with your soul. FEEL your childhood pain and embrace it to get UNSTUCK and move forward on the path of ascension.

The issues from this life and past lives will be presented to you in a synchronistic manner by your soul or entourage and *certainly not in anyway you anticipated.*

Frequently you are not even aware you had an issue with what they present, OR you were sure you already handled that issue, years ago. You probably did BUT there is particular parts or perceptions the invisible realm wants you to REVISIT and embrace. So it will be IN YOUR FACE until you are gracious enough to **SEE IT, embrace it** and own ALL the issues you have experienced and felt.

Aspects of you might have carried your pain, suffering or betrayal so that the core personality could continue functioning. When trauma is too shocking for the child's awareness to absorb, bits of awareness split off. Now might be a goodtime to feel their message and what they felt. Those bits of awareness protected you and took on what you were too fragile and traumatized to INTEGRATE INTO your awareness. A child will get angry, dissociate or depressed about their trauma to protect them FROM the **emotion** that is too overwhelming to absorb and process.

ANGER is a protection or catalyst. Ask your entourage or soul to help take away the dissociation, anger sadness or worthlessness you felt. When you have integrated that aspect your entourage can take the emotional upset out of your DNA. Your inner childhood or discarded bits want to be embraced, heard and melded with the rest of you.

The long-suffering parts of you want the adult's love and compassion. After the melding there might be awareness' or disturbing dreams you never had before. That would be the melded bit trying to share with you how it was for them. Just own that information as part of your total experience. They are just sharing as all healthy children do, listen and love them. They are offering their gifts of awareness to you. They are so VERY happy to be home!

INSIDE you will KNOW!

Chapter 2
ENTOURAGE THERAPY

New Psychology

To heal old self-destructive patterns use the **new psychology.** This is the individual working with their entourage or soul in multidimensions to become aware of their STUCK patterns or the wounds they sustained and do not have compassion for yet. We evolve out of stuckness by feeling and having compassion for our wounds.

One of the rules of the game of free will is that your entourage can only answer the questions the human ASKS. By asking the question you show you are ready to know the answer. The invisible realm is always ready to help the little human or 10%er when they ASK for help, awareness and awakening.

ASK and **listen** within for the answers you seek. Then ACT right away on what your light parts have shared. Circumstances or truths can change in minutes or days so a delay in action means things might have changed and what was shared may no longer BE correct.

Your entourage knows your complete personal history in DETAIL. The invisible realm knows your conscious and **unconscious feelings** and understands what elements created the feelings you have or do not know you have. Your entourage knows the direction the soul wants to take the human.

Another example of therapy with your entourage is brought up in this chapter. This is an example like those in my book Sexual Energy.

RUTH

Below is an example of communication between Ruth and her entourage. This shows the speed that things are moving in the crystalline energy. This communication was done in a week during February 2009.

Ruth is a young woman wanting to rescue Jacob. The light parts of her entourage want her to work on LOVING HERSELF and having COMPASSION for herself.

The dark bits of her entourage are trying to get her to sacrifice herself to Jacob. Similar to when a person is drowning and you jump in the water to save them and you do not know how to swim and you both drown. Ruth's dark bits hope she keeps trying to rescue Jacob.

To justify a relationship with Jacob she continues to believe she NEEDS to rescue him at her own expense. Worrying about someone else is a good way to avoid you and avoid loving yourself.

MY AUNT
My aunt always told me how proud she was of me on the phone.

RUTH
I was killing myself in school, taking physical education classes as an undergrad, several classes in English and writing exces-

sive amounts of papers. I had to come up with idea after idea. I was speaking at four conferences a semester. I was supposed to go stay with her when I went to a conference on romantic literature but I was about to collapse and she said she was proud of me on the phone. She didn't really care if I collapsed or not. They all just keep me doing more and more and more.

RUTH questioning her ENTOURAGE
My father is he sorry?
ENTOURAGE

He is only sorry because your mother has "left" the both of you. He cried that day because your mother had finally left him. He wasn't sorry about putting you in the mental hospital because your mother insisted. You were starting to here us back then. You were going between delightful and sad, pleasing and despondent. You were communicating with dead people. Your creativity was being organized and you were working better.

RUTH

BUT I HATED SCHOOL. I didn't have a lunch and I ate fruit snacks while getting dressed for gym. So unhealthy, no rest, honors course this and honors course that. ALL TO GET INTO HARVARD OR YALE OR CORNELL, all so they could be "proud" of me, and THEN they would love me. When my father said the word "potential" when I was 16, I screamed and slammed the door. I HATE THE WORLD POTENTIAL I avoid using that word at all cost.

RUTH

I WAS 16 YEARS OLD and my father isn't sorry my mom left so I had to take care of him. Clean him up in the middle of the night from all his urine and shit. I had to help him with everything. I would get home from school and he would be barking at me before I could get in the door to do this and to do that. He refused to get a home aide because I was there to do it. I have SO MUCH RESENTMENT.

I am just SOMETHING TO BE "PROUD" of to make THEM look good never mind what it cost me and I feel like a failure. No one genuinely loves me and especially me. I am worthless.

ENTOURAGE

You cannot squeeze blood from a turnip. People that cannot love them self cannot love another. There truths as for all dark entities is that CARE TAKING is showing love. You were being forced to show love to your father.

Your uncle loved you, your grandma loved you, and Jacob loves you.

We ALWAYS love you and feel deep compassion for you.

RUTH

I still don't BELIEVE THIS. Because I hear you in what sounds like my own voice I STILL FEEL LIKE IM MANUFACTURING MY OWN PSYCHODRAMA DIALOG.

My father took "business trips" to Canada when I was seven-years-old. We drove all the way to Montreal. I remember being on the road in the back of the station wagon and there would be nothing around. Was that really the road to Canada, to the city of Quebec?

ENTOURAGE No.

RUTH

Why do I cover up my answers with yes's or no's when they are the opposite?

ENTOURAGE

Because you want to believe the opposite, it's easier that way. But that's okay it's all okay.

RUTH

When I was asked if I was raised in a cult family or was government programmed why did I want to lie and say yes?

ENTOURAGE

Being horrifically abused would explain the way you feel and would also explain why Jacob "picked" you to **continue in the world of abuse and evil.** He picked you for the exact opposite reason because you are a light being. It is easier to be FAT, **rude** and OBKNOXIOUSE, **confused** and all over the place, UNFOCUSED and **slovenly.** That way no one knows who you really are including you.

There was **no structure** to your ABUSE, **no real reason.** Satanism and government programming are VERY systematic and structured.

RUTH

Right now, I want to believe that my parents didn't sell me off in Canada because they really loved me and some goodness rose up in them. I don't remember spending a lot of time in the city of Quebec. The tour guide liked me because I was so attentive and wanted to learn all I could about the city and the Canadian people. I wanted to learn French so my father bought me a children's textbook and I practiced speaking French on the water in the restaurant. I was so eager to please. Do I know French?

ENTOURAGE Yes.

RUTH

Did I know French before I went to Canada?

ENTOURAGE Yes.

RUTH

I know my family needed money when I was little. My mother spends and spends and spends. They took luxurious vacations, kept buying cars. We always had a new car and never kept it for every long, expensive foreign car's.

I had a nanny in Canada. She was a young college student. I normally didn't like babysitters. I also had a nanny growing up.

There wasn't any organization to my abuse. Everyone wanted me when I was little. My aunt would hide me in her over-

Your Entourage is Waiting for you to find them

coat and try to take me home after a party at my parent's house. People showered me with gifts, even my uncle. Why would my mother's brother by me a printer, not on my birthday or anything? My father's older sister made me wear matching designer clothes with her. My mother was jealous of the clothes, very jealous. Everyone wanted me but when I got older, the presents stopped coming. I was very nasty to my uncle, I refused to go see people who were dying or sick, I buried my head in books, music and computers.

It started with my parents just leaving me with people or at places. I loved horses and would horse back ride. I'd be left at my instructor's house waiting outside in the cold and dark for someone to come get me. I found out later that my parents used my "social security money" to pay for my horses and lessons and such. THAT DOESNT MAKE SENSE, USING MY SOCIAL SECURITY MONEY TO PAY FOR HORSES?

My mom worked at the hospital I was born in. It was a catholic hospital run by nuns who knew my mother wanted a baby and were counseling a girl who wanted to give her baby up for adoption. Where was I born?

ENTOURAGE

NEW YORK CITY and that is why you want your baby to be born in New York City to start having the truth revealed to you.

RUTH

Was I stolen from my birth mother?

ENTOURAGE Yes.

RUTH

I was born in Mount Sinai hospital in New York City. There is evidence on the Internet of bad things happening at Mt. Sinai's reproductive center.

My parents adopted my brother in the 1970s. They waited until 1980s to adopt me. My father didn't want to adopt more children. He had a son. My mom desperately wanted more children. She wanted a girl. My parents were in there forties, past the age of having children.

Did my parents try to conceive a child between 1970s and 1980s?

ENTOURAGE No.

Yes, your mother molested your brother. That's why he has so many failed marriages. He keeps marrying the same woman, your mom. A nurse, overpowering, demeaning, controls everything about his life.

RUTH

Did my brother molest me?

ENTOURAGE

Yes, because it made him feel powerful. He was jealous of all the attention you received from everyone. He wanted to make you regret it so he demeaned you just like your mother demeaned him. We frequently give what we got in an effort to heal it. He knew what you really were, where you came from.

RUTH

I was smarter than him so I made him feel small and stupid. I would throw away things of his I didn't like. He told me not too long ago that mom and dad didn't really help him out with going to school, not like they helped me.

But he used to take me on adventures. He'd drive me to the top of mountains and we'd see the whole town. Then he loved having a little sister.

Was that real?

ENTOURAGE

Yes. He allowed you, then, to be a child. You giggled. He didn't ask you to do anything, perform any trick, and be a scholar, draw or nothing. He enjoyed you for the child you were.

RUTH my name isn't really Ruth is it?
ENTOURAGE No.
RUTH

I had a name before that? I've tried to remember my name before. I knew I had another name but it is blocked from me. My mother always claims that she named me. My brother wanted to name me Lisa, my father wanted to name me Susan but she decided I would be Ruth.

ENTOURAGE Yes your birth mother named you.

RUTH is my birth mother still alive?
ENTOURAGE

Yes, but she is a prisoner. She was forced to have more children after you. Your family is spread out. She needed the money.

RUTH did my parents pay for me?
ENTOURAGE No.
RUTH because I failed in the experiment?
ENTOURAGE yes.

RUTH
They tried to get my special gifts to work later. That is why I went to Canada?
ENTOURAGE Yes.
RUTH They tried to use me to get money? Did my real name, what my birth mother named me die and that's how I had "social security money"?
ENTOURAGE
They always have tried to use you to get money and you failed in Canada. Yes, sort of. You were supposed to pay off, be exceptional and you never did. Documents were faked. They adopted you. They named you. So they didn't have to forge any of that. But yes there was money. It was very easy to forge documents to get government money.
RUTH
I was categorized as learning disabled. I remember being in a lower level reading group and going to the resource room for math. Was I really disabled?
ENTOURAGE No. The sexual abuse stunted your growth, mentally and otherwise.
RUTH

But when I was put in a higher reading group they found out I wasn't disabled and that's when I went to Canada? I was 6 then.

My mother abused me more. It made her excited.

Yes.

She could spend more money and maybe they could get a vacation house.

I don't want to do anymore tonight. I can see it now.

NEXT DAY RUTH

I am experiencing a lot of unease, nausea and tension right now. I saw it. I saw it. Oh mommy, I love you mommy, oh that feels good oh mommy. Ruth started to masturbate turned on by this and then... NO I WANT RUTH, SHE LOVES ME

The more I clean out the cobwebs in my head the better I get. I can remember what happened to me without tying back into all the "stress tests" I was administered in Canada. Like getting extreme pain in my butt and wee wee area and today I said "ow" for the first time I said ow instead of trying to BEAR all the pain and my whole body released tension and I was happy.

Your Entourage is Waiting for you to find them

My entourage shows me things in the future.

I would like to work with children, tutoring, teaching writing, art or whatever.

I am going to buy Jacob drugs, vicodin and xanax...I know...trust me I know why he does them because I love him and it is his CHOICE to remain an addict. He does it to feel safe and I am crying like I did when my entourage woke me up in the middle of the night and showed me that Jacob didn't have aids and

No one believed me. But I cried so hard because it was the truth and I believed them. The angels woke me up, it happened a few times and I am able to separate the cult abuse, the lying, stealing from others and me, the cheating on me he has done.

I know the multiple personalities, the programming, the drug addiction and his worthiness as a human being and I can change it into love. I can do this just the way I can separate myself from my mother, from all my mother's, from my health problems, from my mind and intelligence, from my genetics and from my anger.

I am aware of my judging, blaming, controlling and my awareness opens up into a vast plain of human compassion and love and my worthiness as a human being.

When Jacob and I went on our trip from New York to Georgia we sat in the car and he was very afraid and I told him he was worthy. I was afraid to think I was worthy too. That trip was for the both of us. I wanted to kill myself, he wanted to kill himself on and on and it was all to show how worthy we are to be loved.

"I feel weird"

ENTOURAGE "Do you feel light headed?"

RUTH "Yeah..."

ENTOURAGE well you haven't eaten in over a day.

RUTH

People coming down off of Heroin generally have sleeping problems. Jacob is back to solid sleeping again. This is a lot more than Heroin.

Why do I know how to give good head?
ENTOURAGE

You've been doing it all your life. Do they still try and control Jacob and me?

ENTOURAGE

Yes both of you on many occasions call yourselves whores, feel like whores, and prostitute yourselves out to get what you need for shelter to get food and drugs.

RUTH

I remember Jacob identifying us both as whores and when the world ends we would both have sex for money in order to survive. But I'm breaking consciousness with that I am setting an energetic example for myself?

ENTOURAGE

Yes, you are doing very well.

RUTH

I weigh a lot. Is that part of me refusing to play the part of the whore? But also my mother tried to make me in her like-image. That is why I masturbate to fat women.

ENTOURAGE

Yes, no one wants you like this, not even you.

RUTH

Both of our mothers felt ugly and stupid next to their husbands even though they came from more "powerful" families than our fathers. So the women used food to fill them self with the love they didn't get from their PARENTS or their husbands. They didn't realize they NEEDED to LOVE and **HAVE COMPASSION for them self.**

Children always love their mothers no matter what. That is the rule they preach. They can do whatever they want and we the children will still love them. They can feel ugly and stupid and we will find them wonderful. Is that programming?

ENTOURAGE **Yes!**

RUTH

Jacob's mom got him diagnosed with ADHD and told him he was stupid and wouldn't help him with schoolwork and she masqueraded herself as a child advocate.

ENTOURAGE **Yes!**

RUTH

Now he thinks he is stupid and can't do anything with his life outside of his programming and the way he looks to give sex for money and favors. His mom keeps him focused on the way he looks, the image so she can use him for herself.

ENTOURAGE **Yes**!

Your mom did and does the same thing with you Ruth. She seduces you with money and tells you how pretty you are.

RUTH

But I fight against it. I HATE BEING TOLD I am PRETTY I hate people paying attention to me like that.

Jacob was told he was raised in a satanic cult town and his parents were and are members. He and his brother were tested as small children and found to be intelligent enough to be trained into government programming.

Now Jacob is acting like a washing machine. He is reacting now as a devolving spin cycle. Then he is devolving. Then in a jerk fashion Jacob is evolving into light matter, spastic, back and forth like Air hockey with centripetal twists like little typhoons, a very advanced washing machine. Washing, rinse cycle, spin cycle and not permanent press but delicates, cold water for now, maybe lukewarm later.

ENTOURAGE

Jacob is PROCESSING and **collecting the facts** he knows and he is putting them together.

RUTH

I got a lot done while Jacob slept. Something positive was going on in his sleep and I was also warned that he will make more of an effort to deny, cover up, lie, drama and do drugs BUT without the energy behind it that he had before. It will be hard for him to fuel his own deception or illusions now.

I was very happy last night and full of love for myself while I was listening to music. Particularly, I was listening to this song "Love thy will be done" and I automatically thought this song reminds me of Jacob and then I said, it is me! Me loving myself!

"Love thy will be done, I can no longer hide, I can no longer run and that gives me the power to keep up the fight"

Awesome feeling and I was transported around to the future.

I understand the statement now that we are all Gods, because what I felt and am still feeling is love for God. Its like my heart has a back door and I am being pulled up into a god-like being. I don't know I'll have to draw it. I had such vivid images of warmth and hearts and the real sense of success, living my purpose.

And then I had a very long dream about Jacob, but he wasn't Jacob. He was, but this is the real Jacob. The one who came into this world and it was much easier for me to find unconditional love and that is why I was shown him. NOT to judge him but to be able to see more clearly through him. He was considered autistic in my dream because of his intense emotional quality and his very different way of thinking but that's because of whom he is. Someone gave me a lecture in the dream.

"Ruth, Jacob loves you very much but you JUDGE him and TRY to control him. WHAT he needs and WANTS is for you to STOP doing that. Jacob wants your love and support and compassion so he can flower on his own, in his own way and time."

Is that my dark bits speaking?

ENTOURAGE **Yes**.

RUTH

Then Jacob woke up and shrugged off the heroin like it never happened! And then he started dialing his mom who had been calling multiple times the last few days. And my heart jumped a bit because she is not a nice lady and very sexually provocative to her son in his mid twenties.

ENTOURAGE

They told me not to worry, not at all.

RUTH

Why does Jacob sometimes refer to me as a sister?

ENTOURAGE

Because he doesn't understand sexual love or family love or unconditional love he is unable to give his feelings for you a name or word. The closest word he can match to **his** feelings is SISTER. BUT when he has sexual feelings for you he gets conflicted. Jacob feels sex with you would ruin you so he refrains as long as he can. BUT sex is the only way he knows how to relate to others. As "sister", it is easier for him to protect you. YES, the reality is he cannot even care for himself.

RUTH

There are fine lines in memory, in justice, in compassion. Which ones do you cross when it comes to telling someone the

Your Entourage is Waiting for you to find them

truth? When they don't care, when they'd rather join in the fun of it or self-destruction of it? Then you take that step back and just care for yourself, not even waiting for the right time. In that time fold inside yourself, (time is inside of us and in the world really presented and working like a weird origami), if there is a junction of events and the circadian motions of our self to meet in light then so be it. Human alignment among the fine lines of social structures where we will rectify our hearts.

I can only rectify my own heart within itself, origami spatter into some divine spin of soul paint. I can only stand straight for myself. But I think when fine lines become so "jarred" with satanic ritual abuse and programming and any sort of abuse and that a breaking point is coming. A programming crashing!

ENTOURAGE

Always tell the truth, it is good practice for living in the fifth dimension.

RUTH

"What do I get from Jacob?"

ENTOURAGE

He awakened you, brought you to see who you are in this world from the problems with both your mother's to awareness that your heart is shut down and you treat Jacob as your mother treats males. She vents on them all.

Yes, you will write but you are basing it on incorrect things. You write to force others and you keep everyone at a safe distance, you vent all the time as your mom does.

Jacob is right when he says you do not see him. The conditioning you got as a child is that men are to be SERVICED. It is hard for you to see past that and as an adult you pick those types of men so you can SEE your pattern.

You are starting too. Believe in yourself, in your awareness, in your heart, that's where we are and the truth is.

What do I do about the business?
ENTOURAGE

Just take it easy right now. Your drawing with fluidity and meshing your colors and that brings you closer to us and closer to decoding our message. You didn't perceive or honor the quality or effect of the drawing as an "achievement" or "accomplishment." Others perceive your creativity as an accomplishment but you see only a grade on the scale of human effort.

Your narrow view is a reflection of where you are right now.

Your heart is shut down and we are helping you open your heart and use your feelings instead of the third dimensional logic you use to beat people up with. The heart started as a black dot, extending out into the brown and is right now in a sea of green and blue. Then we will help you pull it through the red, orange and yellow. On the top of your painting where it is all yellow, it says "let there be light in this lifetime."

RUTH

My birth mother got slapped as she was losing consciousness during my birth. They yanked me out of her. She underwent electro shock therapy and a variety of other stress tests while I was in the womb right up until I was out of the womb.

They nuked my vagina and my anus all the time causing internal burning inside my intestines. That made me more prone to

PH imbalance and infection in my vaginal area.

I can see a doctor in his office signing papers, receiving immense funding from the Canadian government for these genetic experiments that are linked to stress levels concerning health around the time I was born.

I am tired because my mother used to anesthetize me with chamomile tea. So much herbal tea as a baby and a child made me far more prone to hormonal, gland imbalances. Why do I feel sad?

ENTOURAGE

Ruth, your way of doing this will take longer because you are dragging yourself over hot coals of why why why why why and are CONTROLLING what you feel still! You want to control how you feel it. You are breaking yourself so you can get all of this stuff out of you and move on but you can't do it by yourself, you can't and we are sorry for that. You want to scream and yell and howl, have a big production and then say see I am better. You LOVE DRAMA and have mistaken drama for emotion.

DRAMATIZATION and pretend emotion is a substitute for AUTHENTIC emotions. DRAMATIZATION is repeating an **UNRESOLVED** action that one has experienced in the past. A replay of what happened in the past to get clarity and understanding. The degree of dramatization is in direct proportion to the amount of stuck energy you have in a trauma you experienced. The stuck energy demands you repeat the emotion of the trauma so it can be acknowledged and released. This is definitely NOT in PRESENT time.

Drama protects and prevents the human from feeling *his or her OWN feelings in present time*. Our **true feelings** are in service to us. Owning the truth of your thoughts and feelings keeps them in useful service to you by not letting you IGNORE wounds from your past. Staying in the present moment, facing your feelings of fear and moving into SOLUTIONS and *resolutions* help the individual and the collective dissipate their wounds.

RUTH

I can't understand how to let go! **I cant!** I always have to know why and understand things, **always** ALWAYS always. It gives me a sense of control that I have fought for since I was a fetus and in past lifetimes. I FEEL LIKE IM LOSING CONTROL AGAIN.

With my mother, NO FREE WILL
ENTOURAGE

Let go of your head! Your awareness of love and compassion for your self WILL COME BACK TO YOU.

You won't trust us. You think we are trying to cast a spell on you to love Jacob. That is the fearful little human. You are defining and controlling your love to oh well he needs me to save him.

RUTH

Are you the dark bits of my entourage?

ENTOURAGE, **yes**.
ENTOURAGE

Jacob does not need you to save him; Jacob is the ONLY one that can save Jacob. You love him in a third dimensional CONDITIONAL way. You feel most compassionate toward Jacob when he opens up to you and tells you his sad sad stories. Your heart lights up and you wanted to reach out and hold him but instead you HELD back. Thinking it might be a trick.

RUTH

I was afraid that when I touched him we would have sex. I see I am STILL PEDDLING HUMAN DRAMA AND TRYING TO ANALYZE IT AND MAKING UP VOICES IN MY HEAD TO ENCOURAGE ME TO PEDDLE THROUGH MORE HUMAN BULLSHIT. And I have already created a retort for myself on that.

ENTOURAGE

If you want to stop for now, you can. We don't want you to abuse yourself.

RUTH

WE WOULD HAVE SEX and it would no longer be about human compassion, it would be about sex. Rub rub rub your heart gently down the stream Merrily merrily merrily merrily life is not just a dream! I see all the innuendos and metaphors and analogies. All the perversions of words like rub and stream. I have always seen those things. I FEEL RAPED ALL THE TIME. THATS WHY I HAVE TO DOMINATE OR ELSE I GET VERY CLOSED OFF AND CAN'T INSERT THE PENIS INTO THE VAGINA. Jacob has to dominate to get his orgasm. It is a sexual relationship based on a balance of dominance, 97% of the time. Why is this so hard?

ENTOURAGE

They turned your creativity against you, to the point where your mind is eating itself alive. BLAME JUDGE DAMNATION. That's why you had breakdowns in school writing papers. You could never be perfect. THE MESSAGE IN YOUR brain is you need to be PERFECT to be loved.

You cannot fit the message of heart love heart love heart love into any system so it can be used by that system. Heart love creates its own things. Heart love cannot be used or utilized; anyone who claims that it can does not understand compassion.

You are starting to understand compassion.

Your mother demanded love from you, took what SHE thought was love from you. She forced you to pretend it so she could justify her endless DEMANDING sexual favors from you.

RUTH

THEY KNEW WHAT THEY WERE TAKING FROM JACOB, THEY KNEW. But why would he have so much love in him still even after all of that? WHY IS MY MIND SO WARPED? WHY CANT I SEE THIS CLEARLY AND ORGANIZED?

ENTOURAGE

You were never given any good organization or structure or clarification. Your life was based on other people's DEMANDS. You needs and wants were of no importance to them. You had very rudimentary abuse. Lots of shrieking, hating, excessive fake "love", like a bad soap opera. That's why you refuse to be in touch with your feelings you don't trust them because they were rejected, ignored and you got punished for having them.

RUTH

My grandmother was dying in nursing home. I went and got a nice cool cloth and wiped her face and hands making her more comfortable. She couldn't speak anymore, only made noise, BUT THE WAY SHE LOOKED AT ME; she was sorry, so sorry and was very loving. She had been freed.

How did I know to do that?

ENTOURAGE

Haven't you serviced all your family members and cared for their needs MOST of your childhood?

RUTH

Everyone in my family demanded from me. Why have only certain ones been sorry?

ENTOURAGE

They were awakened. They saw what they had done.

RUTH

I understand what you were saying about children going off into another realm to escape. Jacob does that through music and movies. And I did it with books, music and drama as a child. It is a strange feeling, rotating, revolving consciousness so the same things, like music, have greater meaning to you but less importance like I don't need to bury myself in music to hide or use it to access myself by quoting lyrics instead of **saying what I feel.**

I used to say I felt my outsides—the way I looked—didn't match my insides, because the way I looked was a thing, an object to everyone around me. So I went through radical transformations on the way I looked from not bathing, not brushing my hair, to grunge to pin stripe pants, face paint and princess Leia buns and wearing all black to just giving up period, which was when the confusion and frustration peaked.

But when I was very young, I thought our outsides did match our insides. That when you look in the mirror, really look, you see yourself, the body, as merely an expression of your soul.

Now when someone views me as an object, "oh how pretty you are", I will ignore them instead of letting myself feed into it. But if someone actually looks at you and sees you, then that is a different story.

Jacob does see me from time to time but it's too painful for him, because when he does, I'm usually being myself for a moment, free and in soulful expression. And he realizes for that one small bit that he wants to be the same way, free and soulful.

It feels like I'm dying a little.
ENTOURAGE
Yes, the old Ruth is DYING, grieve her.
RUTH, I puked all over the carpet, what is that all about?
ENTOURAGE

You puked when you were a day or two old. You have developed the habit of puking when things do not make sense to you and that happens often to you. Puking takes your mind off your confusion.

You need to give up trying to CONTROL Jacob, as your mom controlled you. Focus on you and what you need to do. Allow Jacob to do what he needs to do. He is trying to do something for himself and this is how he does it. He is having a hard time right now and you need to allow that without insisting he take care of your needs. His cult and government programming are crashing and you Ruth are being forced to let go so the energy can be transmuted into something new.

RUTH

I think I only understood that in theory about letting go and respecting another person's process and rebalancing.

ENTOURAGE

"Its okay, its okay. Will you be with us now? Will you be with **yourself?** Let Jacob be with Jacob now. You be with us. Its not that he doesn't love you, he doesn't love himself and that is the part he can't figure out and he wants very much to do things for himself. He is going to get mad at everyone and everything. Just be patient."

RUTH

You told me on Friday that Jacob was coming back and that his programming was crashing and I was so happy. I got a lot of work done. Saturday, Sunday and Monday I seemed to be teetering. And now I don't want to believe you about anything!!!! I feel like I'm being punished.

ENTOURAGE

You NEED to give up control, even of yourself. Let us guide you and take care of you.

RUTH

I feel like I'm going through an exorcism. You showed me on Friday about giving up control and letting go but I was scared, **very scared.**

ENTOURAGE

There isn't even a suspicion from our perspective that Jacob doesn't love you. He does and he saw how hard you were trying to take care of yourself when he was here. He is trying to do the same for himself and yes, that does mean taking away control from you, even if he does drugs and sends nude photos of himself, etc.

RUTH Why does it hurt?

ENTOURAGE

Because you are letting go and respecting him and what he wants and in turn you are respecting yourself and what you want. This is the beginning of what love and a relationship is about in the crystalline energy.

RUTH I just had the feeling of wanting to kill myself.

ENTOURAGE

We know, oh we know. But you see you are so much stronger than you think you are AND not even in the way you think you are strong. You are strong because you listen to us and do what's right, not because you can BEAR IT and take on other people and carry them around.

Through the drama tonight, you asked us outright can I call and we said yes, but ONLY if you say Jacob, I'm giving you the computer and mean it and not set it up so you can control it. Let it go and you did and he didn't answer so you said I want to not hold onto this energy anymore over the computer so you sent him an email. And you want it to be over with your parents so get rid of the credit card as soon as you can. Letting go of control and letting go of being controlled. THOSE ARE REALLY BIG STEPS.

RUTH

I want to apologize to everyone for being such a nuisance with all my dramas.

ENTOURAGE

You aren't getting validation and security anymore from outside sources. You will get validation from yourself now. You can get it from yourself. I know you think you are an automaton but when have you seen that? When you stop loving yourself, listening to us and just become a servicing bot.

Ruth

So the reason I'm here is to focus on me, love me, be a grown up, not go running around the country like a chicken with its head cut off. I have the strong urge to run, to flee and go hide out with one of my friends and leave this state to break ties with Jacob, to not be needed or to need him, but that's not the way to go about it, is it?

The new energy makes me very uncomfortable, anxious and I vomit etc. I always assume the worst, that he hates me, that I'm stuck here until doomsday. That he hates me that is why he is not calling. And I am even backing off of that a little. I treat myself that way because I'm assuming about the other person and refuse to listen or understand what is true.

ENTOURAGE

What is going on with Jacob is not as bad as it seems. He is annoyed with everyone right now, but even he knows he is transitioning and like you it makes him uncomfortable, anxious, ill, etc.

He doesn't know HOW to love you or himself. He hasn't been honest with himself yet. His love for you has lead him to start seeing himself. Just be patient with him but mostly with yourself and rise in your own CONSCIOUSNESS.

RUTH

Is this from my dark bits?

ENTOURAGE, **Yes.**

Your Entourage is Waiting for you to find them

ENTOURAGE UPDATE

Your entourage is made up of aspects of YOU. Most of our parts are invisible. Those aspects have different vibrations of awareness and some are dark or light and many shades of gray. Historically we felt we could send the dark gray and black off someplace or wall it off in some way.

That is not the way the universe works.

That is why the human MUST DISCERN what is coming from their light bits and what is coming from their dark bits. Because we are functioning in a free will zone. We are responsible for all our aspects, the dark, gray and light with all their various vibrations of awareness. You need to be aware of the aspect within your entourage answering you questions and what vibration of awareness they are coming from if you care to evolve spiritually.

The human is to DECIDE which aspect or vibration they want to follow the dark, gray or light suggestions.

NOT deciding means you will be controlled or guided by the strongest aspect of you. It is your choice. You can CHOOSE to give your power away.

When you want to make daily LIGHT choices you will need to be very alert at first until you get the hang of it. The human is also RESPONSIBLE for educating their dark aspects and bring them to the light way of reasoning and viewing choices.

When talking to your entourage and asking for guidance and they suggest you DO rescue another, ASK is this coming from the DARK bits of me?

They will say YES if that is true.

You need to pick your direction.

KNOW you are not the victim of any outside source or energy; you carry the darkness within you to understand contrast. When you ask your entourage a question and suspect the dark bits are supplying the answers. Some of us avoid or deny this much honesty and will say, "I can't hear." Generally that is a YES or your question is too broad for them to answer.

Ask just one question at a time so the answers are clear to you.

Your ENTOURAGE is WAITING for you to find them.

Who or what are you listening too.
What or who are you guided by.
Have you considered listening to your entourage?

Chapter 3
Svali Speaks

http://www.mindcontrolforums.com/svali_speaks.htm

Svali has her entire book on the Internet and I am only taking some of her work in this chapter.

About the author: Hi, my name is Svali. My entire family and I were involved in a cult group until several years ago, when we broke free. I used to be a programmer in the cult, and now I want to share the knowledge that I have to help others. I am also a writer, and a registered nurse. I currently work as a diabetic educator in Texas.

Equipment Frequently Used by Trainers: The cult has become quite technologically advanced. **Training room:** the average training room is a neutral colored room, with walls painted, either a dull gray, white, or beige. Some may be painted in various colors, as part of color-coding. They are often located in secret underground rooms, or basements of large private residences, and will be entered from the main building through a covered doorway. Impromptu training rooms may be setup during military exercises outdoors, in covered canvas tents.

Trainers: the Illuminati have a rule: there must always be a minimum of two trainers working with a person. This prevents a trainer from being either too severe, or permissive, or developing too close a bond with the subject; the watchful eye of the other trainer prevents this. Younger trainers are paired with older, more experienced trainers. The older trainer will teach the younger, who does most of the actual work. If the younger is unable to finish a task, or loses heart, the older one will step in.

Head trainers: will teach, they will also work with the council leaders and hierarchy. All members are required to come in for a "tune up" (reinforcing programming), even top leaders, from time to time.

EEG machine: will often have abbreviated hookups for quick use. Used extensively with brain wave programming; also to

Your Entourage is Waiting for you to find them

verify that a certain alter is out when called up. May be used to verify deep trance state before initiating deep programming. Trainers are taught to read these readouts.

Trainer's table: a large table, frequently steel covered with plastic, or easily cleaned material. On the sides at intervals are restraints for arms, legs and the neck to prevent movement. Trainer's chair: large chair with arm rests. Will have restraints as above at intervals to restrain movement while person sits in chair. **Shock equipment:** models and types are quite varied, depending on age and company. Most have a set of rubber-covered wires, with electrodes that may be connected with Velcro, rubber (steel tips imbedded under finger and toe nail beds), or gel pads (larger body areas such as chest, arms, legs). Some are tiny electrodes, which can be taped next to eyes, or placed within genitalia. These are connected to the "shock box", which has controls that can determine amount of electricity, and frequency, if interval shocks are desired.

Drugs: any number of opiates, barbiturates, hypnotics, sedatives, and anesthetic agents. Resuscitative drugs, antidotes are also kept, clearly labeled and indexed. Many drugs, especially experimental ones, are only known by code names, such as "alphin 1".

CPR equipment: in case person has adverse reaction to drugs or programming. At times, a child alter will come out inadvertently during a programming sequence, and will be overdosed with the drugs meant for adult alters. The trainers must give it the antidote, and resuscitate it, just as if a real child is out. They are well aware of this fact, and will severely punish child altars, to teach them to come out only when called out.

Virtually reality headsets: the keystone in recent years. Many programming sequences utilize holographic images, and virtual reality set ups, including assassination programs, where the person realistically "kills" another human being. These virtual disks are far more advanced than those in video arcades.

Body building equipment: used in military training to increase fitness, lean body mass.

Steel instruments: used to insert into orifices to cause pain

Stretch machine: used as punishment, "stretches" person without breaking bones extremely painful.

Trainer's grids and projectors: used to project grids on wall or ceiling.

Movie projector: to show movies, although new VR disks are replacing these computer: collect and analyze data; keep computer grid on person's system. Current military computer access codes will be used to download into governmental computers.

Trainer's Journals: contain indexed copies of subject's systems, including key alters, command codes, etc.

Comfort objects: used to comfort subject afterwards. May be toy or candy for child alters, or oils for massage. Warm towels, or beverages may be given, as the trainer "bonds with" and comforts person they worked with. This is probably the most important part of the training process, as the trainer explains calmly, kindly how well the person did, how proud they are of them.

Overview of the Illuminati to understand Illuminati cult programming, it is first necessary to understand a bit about the structure and philosophy of the organization. They follow a philosophy known as "Illuminism" or "enlightenment". The Illuminati were named several hundred years ago, but trace their roots and history to the ancient mystery religions of Egypt, ancient Babylon, and even Mesopotamia. Out of these ancient religions, which were practiced secretly over hundreds and hundreds of years, there arose esoteric groups, which continued to practice the rites, traditions, and enculturation brought in from the original groups.

Some of the groups, which came out of these ancient roots, included the order of the Knights Templar, Rosicrucian's, Baphetomism, and Druidic cults.

The original Illuministic leaders chose to take what they felt were the best practices of each root religion, combine them into principles then organized these principles. Modern day Illuminism is a philosophy funded by the wealthy, but practiced in all social strata. It is a philosophy whose tenets have spread across the world. It started with the German branch of Rosicrucian's, spread to England, and then came to the United States with the first settlers.

The Illuminati have 3 main branches: the Germanic branch, which oversees the others, the British branch, which handles finances, and the French/Russian branch. All 3 branches are represented in the United States and Canada, as well as every country in the world. The top levels are known as:

Hierarchical level The Illuminati have divided the United States into 7 geographical regions; each region has its own regional council, composed of 13 members, with an advisory board of 3 elders to each one. These regions interact for purposes of finances; personnel; teaching, etc. Beneath each regional council, is a local council of 13 members, the head of whom sits on the regional council, and gives it information about the local groups underneath his leadership.

HOW THE ILLUMINATI MAKE MONEY There are several illegal enterprises that they are involved in, as well as legal ones.

Drug running: The Illuminati linked up with the Mafia and the Columbians, years ago, to help each other out with bringing drugs into the United States. They also provide couriers for taking drugs and money out of the States. The Illuminists are generally wealthy businessmen, who have 4 layers of people underneath them. The fourth layer down actually has contact with the people in the drug industry. They never identify themselves as Illuminists; only as people interested in investing, with a guaranteed profit, and are highly secretive.

Pornography: The Illuminati are linked in pornography/prostitution/child prostitution/ and white slavery sales. Again, several layers are present, as a buffer, between the true "management" and those either engaged in the activities, or in paying for/funding and eventually being paid for the activities.

Children: are often supplied from the local cult groups, and taught to be child prostitutes (and later, adult prostitutes); are photographed and filmed in every type of pornography available, including "snuff films" and violent films.

Gun running: The Illuminati and other groups are also involved in international gun sales and shipments.

Buying access codes for military computers: The Illuminati will have people from all strata of civilian life trained to go and make pickups near or on military bases. A typical person used might be the innocent looking wife of military person, a local businessman, or even a college student. The Illuminists like having access to military computers, because that will gain them entrance to closed files the world over.

Hiring and selling assassinations: this is done worldwide, more in Europe than in the States. These people are paid big money to do either a private or political assassination.

Mercenaries/military trainers: guess who gets paid money to come in and train paramilitary groups? Who has training camps all over the states of Montana, Nevada, and North Dakota?

Banking: The original Illuminists were bankers, and they have highly trained financiers to organize their money, and funnel the above illicit funds into more "respectable" front groups/organizations. They will also start charities, community organizations, etc., as fronts.

Jobs in the Illuminati (or Why They Spend All That Time Training People) To understand generational programming, it helps to understand WHY the cult goes to the amount of trouble that it does to place programming into people. Training represents TIME and EFFORT, and no one- especially a cult member- will spend that amount of energy unless there will be a return on the investment. People who are well trained in their jobs- so well trained, that they can **do their tasks without even thinking about them.** To maintain secrecy, this group must also have people completely dedicated to not revealing their roles in the cult- even under threat of death or punishment. The cult wants members who are completely loyal to the group and its tenets, who never question the orders they are given. These qualities in-group members ensure the continuance of the cult.

Informers: These people are trained to observe details and conversations with photographic recall. They will download large amounts of information under hypnotic trance. Detailed knowledge of conversations or even documents can often be retrieved in this manner.

Breeders: These people are often chosen from childhood to have and breed children. They may be chosen according to bloodlines, or given in arranged marriages or cult alliances, to "elevate" the children. A parent will often sell the services of a child as a breeder to the local cult leader.

Prostitutes: Prostitutes can be a male or female of any age. They are trained from earliest childhood to give sexual favors to one or more adults in return for payment to the child's parents or their local cult group.

Pornography A child used in pornography (which may include bestiality) can also be of any age or sex. Child pornography is also big business in the

Cult, and includes snuff films.

Media personnel These are very bright, verbal people. They will be sent to journalism school and will work for local or regional media upon graduation. They write books and articles sympathetic to the Illuministic viewpoint without ever revealing their true affiliation. They do biased research in their articles, favoring only one viewpoint, such as denying the existence of DID or ritual abuse.

Preparers: set up tables, cloths, candles, and paraphernalia quickly and efficiently. This job is learned from infancy on.

Readers: read from the book of Illumination or local group archives; they also keep copies of sacred literature in a safe vault and are trained in ancient languages.

Cutters: are taught to dissect animal or human sacrifices (they are also known as the "slicers and dicers" of the cult). They can do a kill quickly, emotionlessly, and efficiently. They are trained from early childhood on.

Chanters: sing, sway, or lead choruses of sacred songs on high holy occasions.

High Priest/Priestess: The person who holds this job is changed every few years in most groups, although it may be held longer in smaller, more rural groups. These people administrate and lead their local cult group as well as coordinate jobs within the cult.

Trainers: These people teach local group members their assigned jobs and monitor the performance of these jobs at local group meetings.

Punishers These are the people who brutally punish/discipline members caught breaking rules or acting outside of or above their authority and are universally despised by other cult members.

Trackers: These people will track down and keep an eye on members who attempt to leave their local group. They are taught to use dogs, guns and taser.

Teachers: These people teach group classes to children to indoctrinate cult philosophy, languages, and specialized areas of endeavor.

Childcare: These people care for very young children when the adults are at local group meeting. After age two, children are routinely engaged in some form of group activity led by trainers of the youngest children.

Couriers: Run guns, money, drugs, or illegal artifacts across state or national lines. Usually they are people who are young and single without outside accountability.

Commanding officers: These people oversee military training in the local groups and help ensure the smooth running of these exercises.

Behavioral scientists: These individuals often oversee the training in local and regional groups. These students of human behavior are intensely involved in data collection and human experimentation in the name of the pursuit of knowledge of human behavior in the scientific realm.

THE ILLUMINATI PLAN TO RULE THE WORLD

The Illuminists believe that our government, as we know it, as well as the governments of most nations around the world, are destined to collapse. These will be planned collapses, and they will occur in the following ways: The Illuminati has planned first for a financial collapse that will make the great depression look like a picnic. This will occur through the maneuvering of the great banks and financial institutions of the world, through stock manipulation, and interest rate changes. Most people will be indebted to the federal government through bank and credit card debt, etc. The governments will recall all debts immediately, but most people will be unable to pay and will be bankrupted.

Next there will be a military takeover. After the military takeover, the general population will be given a chance to either espouse the Illuminati's cause, or reject it (with imprisonment, pain, even death being possible punishments).

How the Illuminati Program People: An Overview of Some Basic Types of Programming The programming techniques that I will describe take an incredible amount of effort, time, dedication, and planning on the part of the cult to place in the individual. I no longer do these things, nor do I espouse doing them. Unintentional programming versus intentional programming

The programming of a generational Illuminati infant often begins before its birth and the very environment the infant is raised in becomes a form of programming. Often, the infant is raised in a family environment that combines **daytime abandonment** with dysfunction in the parental figures. The infant soon learns that the **nighttime,** and cult activities, is the truly important ones. The infant may be deprived of attention, or even abused, in the daytime; and is only treated as special, or "seen" by the parent, in the cult setting. This can lead to very young alters around the core or core splits, who feel "invisible", abandoned, rejected, unworthy of love or attention, or that they don't even exist, unless they are doing a job for their "family".

Another milieu and conditioning process the infant must face is that the adults around him/her are INCONSISTENT, since the adults in a generational cult family are almost always also multiple, or DID. This sets up a reality for the infant/toddler that the parents act one way at home; an entirely different way at cult gatherings; and yet a different way in normal society. The child has NO CHOICE but to accept this reality.

INTENTIONAL PROGRAMMING Prenatal splitting is well known in the cult, as the fetus is very capable of fragmenting in the womb due to trauma. This is usually done between the seventh and ninth month of pregnancy. Techniques used include: placing headphones on the mother's abdomen, and playing loud, discordant music (such as some modern classical pieces, or even Wagner's operas). Loud, heavy rock has also been used. Other methods include having the mother ingest quantities of bitter substances, to make the amniotic fluid bitter, or yelling at the fetus inside the womb. The mother's abdomen may be hit as well. Mild shock to the abdomen may be applied, especially when term is near, and may be used to cause premature labor, or ensure that the infant is born on a ceremonial holiday.

Certain labor inducing drugs may be also given if a certain birth date is desired. Once the infant is born, testing is begun at a very early age, usually during the first few weeks of life. The trainers, who are taught to look for certain qualities in the infant, will place it on a velvet cloth on a table, and check its reflexes to different stimuli. The infant's strength, how it reacts to heat, cold, and pain are all tested. Different infants react differently, and the trainers are looking for dissociative ability, quick reflexes, and reaction times. They are also encouraging early dissociation in the infant with these tests. The infant will also be abused, to create fragments. Methods of abuse can include: rectal probes; digital anal rape; electric shocks at low levels to the fingers, toes, and genitalia; cutting the genitalia in ritual circumstances (in older infants). **The intent is to begin fragmentation before a true ego state develops,** and customize the infant to pain and reflexive dissociation from pain (yes, even tiny infants dissociate; they will grow blank and limp, or glassy, in the face of continued trauma.) Isolation and abandonment programming will sometimes be begun as well, in a rudimentary sense. The infant is abandoned, or uncared for by adults, intentionally during the daytime, then picked up, soothed, cleaned up and paid attention to in the context of preparing for a ritual or group gathering.

The infant will be taught to associate maternal attention with going to rituals, and eventually will associate cult gatherings with feelings of security.

As the infant grows older, i.e. at 15 to 18 months, having the parents as well as cult members abuse the infant more methodically and intentionally does more fragmenting. This is done by intermittently soothing, bonding with the infant, then shocking it on its digits; the infant may be dropped from heights to a mat or mattress and laughed at as it lays there startled and terrified, crying. It may be placed in cages for periods of time, or exposed to short periods of isolation. Deprivation of food, water, and basic needs may begin later in this stage. All of these methods are done in order to create intentional dissociation in the infant. The infant of this age may be taken to group meetings, but outside of special occasions, or dedications, will have no active role yet in the cult setting. The small infants are usually left with a cult member, or caretaker, who watches them during the group's activities; this caretaker role is usually rotated among lower level or teenage members.

Between the ages of 20 and 24 months, the toddler may begin the "steps of discipline" or "steps of torment and abuse" which the Illuminati use to teach their children. The age the child begins them will vary, depending upon the group, the parent, the trainer, and the child. There purpose is to create a highly dissociative child, out of touch with their feelings, who is completely and unthinkingly loyal to the cult. Most follow this outline at least roughly.

First step: to not need The small toddler/child is placed in a room without any sensory stimulus, usually a training room with gray, white, or beige walls. The adult leaves and the child is left alone, for hours, to an entire day.

If the child begs the adult to stay or screams, the child is beaten, and told that the periods of isolation will increase until they learn to stop being weak. The ostensible purpose of this discipline is to teach the child to rely on its own internal resources, and not on outside people. What it actually does is create a huge terror of abandonment within the child. When the trainer, returns to the room, the child is often found rocking itself, or hugging itself in a corner, occasionally almost catatonic from fear. The trainer will then "rescue" the child, feed and give it something to drink and bond with the child as their "savior". The trainer will tell them the "family" told the trainer to rescue the child, because its family "loves" it. The trainer will instill cult teachings, at this point, into the helpless, fearful, and almost

Your Entourage is Waiting for you to find them

insanely grateful child who has just been "rescued" from isolation.

The trainer will reinforce in the child over and over how much it "needs " its family, who just rescued it from death by starvation or abandonment. This will teach the very young toddler to associate comfort and security with bonding with its trainer, who may be one of its parents, and being with "family" members. The cult is very aware of child developmental principles, and has developed exercises like the above after hundreds of years of teaching very young children.

Second step: to not want This step is very similar to the first step, and actually reinforces it. It will be done intermittently with the first step over the next few years of the child's life. An adult will enter the room, with a large pitcher of ice water or food. If the child asks for either, as the adult is eating or drinking in front of the child, he/she is severely punished for being weak and needy. This creates in the child a hyper-vigilance as she/he learns to look for outside adults for cues on when it is okay to fulfill needs, and not **to trust her/his own body**

signals. Third step: to not wish The child is placed in a room with favorite toys, or objects. A kind adult comes into the room and engages the child in play. The child and adult may engage in fantasy play about the child's secret wishes, dreams, or wants trust is slowly gained. At some later point, the child is severely punished for any aspect of wishing or fantasy shared with the adult, including the destruction of favorite toys, going in and undoing or destroying secret safe places the child may have created, or even destroying non cult protectors. This step is repeated, with variations, many times over the ensuing years. This step creates in the child the feeling that there is no true safety that the cult will find out everything it thinks.

Fourth step: the survival of the fittest This step is used to create perpetrator alters in the young child. ALL CULT MEMBERS WILL BE EXPECTED TO BECOME PERPETRATORS; THIS BEGINS IN EARLY CHILDHOOD. The child is brought into a room where there is a trainer and another child of approximately the same age, or slightly younger, that the child being taught. The child is severely beaten, for a long period of time, by the trainer, then told to hit the other child in the room, or they will be beaten further. If the child refuses, it is punished severely, the other child is punished as well, and then the child is told to punish the other child. If the child continues to refuse, or cries, or tries to hit the trainer instead, they will continue to be beaten severely, and told to hit the other child, to direct its anger at the other child. This step is repeated until the child finally complies. This step is begun around age 2 to 2 1/2, and is used to create aggressive perpetrator alters in the young child. They will also be mimicking adults, who role model perpetration constantly as normal.

Fifth step: the code of silence Many, many different stratagems are used to put this in, starting at around the age of two years old, when a child starts becoming more verbal. Usually, after a ritual or group gathering, the child is asked about what they saw, or heard, during the meeting. Like most obedient young children, they will comply. They are immediately severely beaten, or tortured, and a new alter is created, who is told to keep or guard the memories of what was seen, on pain of their life. The child will be exposed to setups and role-plays throughout their growing up that reinforce this step.

Colors, Metals and Jewel Programming Color coding One form of programming that is quite common in the Illuminati is color programming. Why is it done? The answer is that trainers are human, and also quite lazy. Color programming is a simple way to organize systems, and allows the trainer to call up alters easily within a system. With the thousands of fragments that many multiples in the cult have, colors are a way of organizing them into an easily accessible group. Also, young children recognize colors before they can read, so this training can occur quite early.

It is begun at about age two in most children. How it is done: The child is taken into a room with, white, beige, or colored walls. If the room is a neutral color, the lights in the room will be changed, so they color the room with the light's color. If "blue" is the color being imprinted, or put in, the trainer will call up a young child alter, either a controller or core split for a system. They will tell the child that they will learn how to become blue, and what blue means. The room will be bathed in blue light, as mentioned, or has been painted blue for use in this kind of programming. The trainer will be dressed in blue clothing, and may even have a blue mask on. Blue objects will be placed around the room. The alter inside the child is called up, drugged, hypnotized, and traumatized on the table. As they are awakening from the trauma, still in trance, they are told that blue is good, and that they are blue. That blue is important. That blue will protect them from harm. That blue people don't get hurt. This will go on for a while.

They then ask the child if they want to be "blue", like the trainers. If the child says yes, they will continue on. If the child says no, it will be re-traumatized until it says yes. The child is often naked, and told it cannot wear clothing until it "earns" the right to wear beautiful blue clothing. Over and over the "safety of being blue" (i.e. freedom from harm) and danger of not having a color is emphasized. They are drugged, hypnotized, traumatized, while the meaning of blue is ground in over and over. They are forced to act in "blue" ways.

If the trainer at a later date wants to access a blue system, they may call them up by color, or wear a piece of clothing or a scarf in the color they want to reach. This becomes an unconscious trigger for this color to come forward. **Metals programming:** is a type of programming that many Illuminati children are given. Because it is so similar to jewels programming, I will discuss how it is done under jewels. Metals can be from bronze (lowest) to platinum (highest).

Jewels programming: Jewels is considered higher than metals, and more difficult to obtain. Which is put in and when, is dependent on the child's status, its parents status, the region it is born in, the group it is born into, and the trainers that work with it.

The child is shown a piece of jewelry such as a ring, or else a large example of the jewel (or metal) being put in. They are asked: "isn't this Amethyst, or Ruby, Emerald, Diamond) beautiful?" The child will be eager to look at it, touch it, and is encouraged to by a trainer with a soft kind voice.

Your Entourage is Waiting for you to find them

The trainer will ask the child, "wouldn't you like to be beautiful, like this jewel? (Or metal jewelry)". The training often begins between ages two and three. The child is then told that in order to become a jewel, they must "earn the right". This involves passing "special tests" going through the rungs of the long, arduous training process expected of Illuminati children; having a jewel or metal involves stepping up in status and being praised. But the price is enduring hours of abuse called "training" but in reality is organized, systemic abuse to make the child do what the trainer wants them to become. Over time, with the help of drugs, hypnosis, shock, and other trauma, as the child goes through it's training process, it will begin earning its jewels and/or metals, one by one. These will become full alters inside. **Amethyst** is usually the first one earned, and is linked to keeping secrets. **Ruby** will often be next, and is linked to sexual abuse and sexual alters inside. As the child is repeatedly sexually traumatized and survives, or creates sexual alters to please adults, they are "rewarded" by being allowed to become a ruby.

Emerald will often come later (ages 12 to 15). This is considered very precious, and is linked to family loyalty, witchcraft, and spiritual achievement. Emeralds will often have a black cat, or "familiar" linked to them.

Diamond is the highest gemstone, and not all children will earn it.

"Family jewels" are often passed down internally during training sessions with trainers and family members. All high Illuminati families will have jewels hidden in secret vaults (real, outside jewels), which have been passed down for generations.

Brain Wave Programming depends on several factors. These include: the child's ability to dissociate; the region of the country or which country the child grows up in; the level of ability of the trainers the child has contact with; physical resources and equipment available. There is no one "recipe" that fits every person. Brain wave programming involves having a young child go into a deep trance state, where they then learn to dissociate into a certain brain wave pattern. This is a complex skill, and not all children can achieve this. The goal is for the child to reach, for example, a consistent delta state, where delta brain waves show up on the EEG,

Usually, two or even three trainers will work on one child during the initial stages. One will "prep" the child, using a hypnotic drug to induce a trance state. They will have also placed the electrodes on the head, using an abbreviated version of the method used in traditional hospital setting. If delta state is being induced, only the electrodes needed to pick up delta waves will be placed, for example. This is to save time.

The average child is about eight years old when this is begun, since the cerebral cortex and neurological development are not advanced enough at earlier ages (It has been tried at earlier ages, quite unsuccessfully, in the past; this practice was dropped because of the neurological damage and "failure to take rate" that trainers were seeing). The non-prepping trainer will then let the child know exactly what he/she expects: that they will achieve a special state, called "delta state". The trainer tells the child, while they are in trance state that they will know when they reach it, by the readings from the electrodes.

The trainer will tell the child alter, who has been called up to be a "template", or building block for the new system, that delta is good. They will emphasize this over and over. The child will then be shocked to increase its receptivity to learning. This also arouses the child from its drugged state and it will be more alert. It will want to please the trainer. The trainer will tell the child that she/he wants it to perform certain mental exercises. It will then give it backwards counting exercises, used to help the child achieve deeper trance states. The trainers will now have a template that stays always in delta state, that they can begin splitting and using as the basis of forming a new system inside.

Common brain wave states used are:
Alpha: this is the most easily reached brain wave state, and also includes both the youngest and most easily accessed alters in the entire system. Young children have long periods of alpha activity and must be trained to enter other brain wave states for long periods. System access programming;

Your Entourage is Waiting for you to find them

access codes and sexual alters will often be placed in alpha, which may also be coded red in some systems.

Beta: this is the next most easily reached state, and is often associated with aggressive impulses. Beta state will often hold cult protectors, internal warriors, and military systems. They may be color coded blue.

Gamma: this will often hold extremely cult loyal alters, and holds more emotion than the other states, except for alpha. Suicide programming will often be layered into this system, as these alters would rather die than leave their "family". Scholarship programming may be held by this system, since they easily memorize by rote. Several languages may be spoken by different alters in this system, as the Illuminati like to program in plural linguality, with up to eight languages, both modern and ancient being spoken.

Delta: this is one of the more cognitive brain wave states, and will often be highly dissociated. It may also be the "ruling" or controlling state over the other brain wave systems. Often, delta state may be configured inside as a computer, and the delta alters will have emotionless, flat alters with photographic memories. They may hold most of the cognitive memories for the other systems, especially if extensive amnesia programming has been done. Delta state may have up to three levels of training: delta 1, delta 2, and delta 3 which will also correlate to security access allowed within the cult; i.e. access to highly confidential information. Behavioral sciences programming may be held by this system. Internal programmers, self destruct, psychotic, and shatter programming as well as other punishment programming sequences to prevent outside access or internal access to the systems may be held within delta systems. It may be color-coded both orange/blue/purple, and will also often be the entry way to higher systems such as jewels or internal councils, inside.

Epsilon: this is often a "hidden system" and may hold CIA programming and high-level governmental programming. Assassin programming may be held in this system, or in the beta system, depending on the trainer. Covert operations, courier operations, learning to tail a subject, or "drop a tag", disguises, getting out of difficult situations, may be handled by this system, which sees itself as chameleon-like. It may be color coded brown.

Phi/Theta/Omega programming: this represents negative spiritual programming. These are the "dark" ritual alters, who participate in blood rituals, sacrifices, and ceremonies. Internal witches, warlocks, seers, psychics, readers, and occult practitioners will be placed in this system, which has highly developed right brain and deep trance abilities. They will often be color coded black. This is an overview of some of the more common brain wave systems. It is often placed in over a matter of years, from ages 8 to 21 being the primary ones, with occasional reinforcement of the programming from time to time.

Brain wave programming is a very complex form of programming, which creates automatic amnesia and communication barriers between the different brain wave states. This will also be reinforced by shock and punishment to prevent its "degradation", or undoing. Internal system controllers and programmers will also work to reinforce the programming, especially at night, when the person is asleep (physically).

All brain wave systems will have system controllers; usually set up in a group of three (the Illuminati love triads, as being the "mystical" and most stable number. They believe that systems built upon triads are extremely strong, unbreakable, and will often program in threes: three back ups, three system controllers, etc.)

Flood programming is a sequence put in place to punish a system if its internal programming is allowed to degrade or access to an unauthorized person, either internally or externally, is allowed. It will involve the fragments that hold highly traumatic memories, both emotional and physical, being pushed to the front where the person is "flooded" with wave after wave of memories. If this is triggered, and it frequently is if the survivor is in therapy, the first priority should be slowing the memories down. This may mean trying to reason with internal controllers or deltas who are allowing the flooding; they need to know that if the front, or previously amnesic alters down, or are re-shattered due to traumatization, it will weaken all the systems.

Military Programming The Illuminati are emphasizing the importance of military training more and more, as part of their plan for eventual takeover. All children in the current generation are undergoing some form of military training as part of this plan often started by three years of age with simple exercises. Their parents take the children to a training area, which may be a large inside auditorium, or a remote area outside where training maneuvers are done. Tents are set up, with command centers for the different commanding officers and military trainers.

The children are taught to march in time, keeping a straight line. They are punished by being kicked, shocked with a cattle prod, or beaten with a baton if they move out of place. They will be dressed in small uniforms in imitation of the adults. The adults will have ranks, badges and insignia indicating their level of achievement in the cult hierarchy and military.

They will spend hours learning to aim, sight, and fire these guns at targets. At first the targets are bulls eyes, but as the children get older the targets will be similar to police cut outs of humans. The children are taught to aim for the head or the heart. Later, they will graduate to realistic manikins. This is conditioning them to kill a human being. They will be shown violent films of warfare, much more explicit and graphic than normal movies in-group classes. Killing techniques will be shown in slow motion. The motif "kill or be killed" will be ground in over and over. Exercises for older youth will include games where groups compete against each other, and the older teen leads, with the help of an adult advisor. Groups that win are rewarded groups that lose are punished. The youth are taught to leave behind the weak, or slow members. Unfit members are shot or killed, and the youth leader learns to do these tasks. They are taught to bring their unit through simulated battles with other units, and cool, cognitive logic under these conditions is rewarded. The goal is to creative cognitive leaders inside the military systems, who are dissociated from emotions under the stress of battle conditions.

CIA, Governmental, and Scholarship programming Some systems will have internal CIA programming. Some of the methods mentioned in earlier chapters, such as brain wave programming and color-coding were developed in part through funding by the CIA in the 1950's and 1960's. Military intelligence officers working in Langley, Virginia, used these government funds to conduct research on human subjects. They reported what they were learning to trainers throughout the U.S. and Europe. CIA programming can include having alters in a system trained in different techniques of both finding a target, and studying the target without being detected. The end result of tagging the victim can include having a sexual assignation with the target, or may involve having people inside trained to assassinate a target.

These are complex programming sequences, and are put in over years of training, with periodic reinforcement. Alters may be trained to become hyper aware of their environment, and able to overhear conversations that are whispered. Internal recorders are taught to download these

conversations, as well as other info. Photographic recall is emphasized, as the person will be hypnotized or put into a delta state for "downloading" information to the trainer or
CIA operative.

Governmental Programming: the person being trained to take leadership positions or administrative positions in the government. They may be trained to network with others in governments local, national, and international. The Illuminati's stated goal is to infiltrate, and eventually cause the downfall of, all major governments in the world. Government operatives are taught to do this by: infiltrating local political parties running for leadership both locally and nationally working for top leaders, as administrators, financial advisors funding governmental races and backing the person sympathetic to the Illuminati, or putting their person in to win, creating political chaos and unrest with operatives trained in dissension. The people selected for governmental programming are usually highly intelligent with native charm, or charisma. They are also skilled people manipulators.

These abilities may be enhanced through programming, encouraging the person to project a "persona" that will draw people to them.

Scholarship training: The Illuminati revere scholarship, especially oral tradition. Children with good memories and native intelligence may undergo specific training in the area of scholarship. This will include learning under trauma, with praise for accomplishment. It will also mean punishment or being shocked for poor performance. Some of the major areas of scholarship include, but are not limited to: Oral tradition: history of the Illuminati, especially the child's particular branch, memorizing genealogies. Learning and becoming fluent in multiple languages, both modern and ancient, including but not limited to: English, French, German, Russian, Spanish, Arabic, Latin, Greek, Hebrew, Egyptian hieroglyphics: ancient Babylonian, ancient Chaldean and cuneiform writings.

Scholarship programming will involve alters who are intensely loyal to the cult, since they believe they are related to a long, unbroken line of people since earliest history. They will often be immersed in cult philosophy, having read and memorized numerous esoteric volumes related to it. Appealing to logic, intellect, having an open mind and discussing the pros and cons of leaving the cult with them will often be received the best. They despise open conflict, and prefer addressing issues intellectually. They will be skilled debaters, and quite verbal. Asking them to read books that address becoming free from the cult, and asking them to sit in and listen to accounts from traumatized alters both in their system and others inside, will often help them make the decision to switch loyalties. Although they will have been immersed in false ideologies and doctrines, they are frequently willing to attempt to be intellectually honest. They will read and debate both sides of an issue, and may become some of the first to make the decision to leave the cult once convinced that it is abusive.

Programming Linked to Stories, Movies, Cartoons, or role

Play Dramatization a special type of programming that is universal with the Illuminati. For countless centuries, Illuminati

Your Entourage is Waiting for you to find them

trainers and leaders have used role-playing to reinforce as well as program children, and it is a favorite mode of teaching up to this day.

How Script programming is done: The trainer will play the movie for the child. The script programming will often be linked to other programming the child is undergoing. Military programming may be linked to Star Wars. Total recall programming may be linked to Data in Star Trek. Computer programming may be linked to Hal in 2001 A Space Odyssey; internal labyrinth programming may be linked to the movie "Labyrinth". The possibilities are quite varied and will depend on both the child and the trainer as to which direction script programming will go. Music from the show, or scene, will be used as a trigger to access the programming inside or bring forward these personalities.

Scripted programming will often involve a great deal of traumatization, to create the "blank slate" alters desired. The programming will be ground in with repetition, electroshock, torture, drugging and hypnosis. The alters inside who have gone through this programming will often be highly disconnected from external reality and may believe that they are part of a "script". They may be Dorothy seeking the Emerald City (or the achievement of Illuminati rule on earth). They may be a computer or the character Data. Reality orientation will be very important.

The Sixth step of Discipline: Betrayal; Twinning, Internal walls,

Structures, Geometry, Betrayal programming will begin in infancy, but will be formalized at around ages six to seven, and continue on into adulthood. The sixth step can be summarized as: "betrayal is the greatest good." The Illuminists teach this to their children as a very important spiritual principle. They idealize betrayal as being the true state of man. The quick witted, the adept, learns this quickly and learns to manipulate it.

The child will learn this principle through set up after set up. The child will be placed in situations where an adult who is kindly, and in set up after set up "rescues" the child, gains its trust. The child looks up to the adult as a "savior" after the adult intervenes and protects the child several times. After months or even a year of bonding, one day in a set up the child will turn to the adult for help. The adult will back away, mocking the child, and begin abusing it. This sets in place the programming: adults will always betray a child and other adults. Another set up will involve twinning, which deserves special mention here. The Illuminati will often create twin bonds in their children. The ideal is to have a set of real twins, but of course this is not always possible. So, the child is allowed to play with, and become close to, another child in the cult from earliest childhood. At some point early on, the child will be told that the other child is actually their "twin", and that they were separated at birth. They are told that this is a great secret and not to tell anyone, on pain of punishment. The child, who is often lonely and isolated, is overjoyed. It has a twin, someone who has a special bond to them by birth. The children do everything together. They are taught together, do military training together. They tell each other secrets. They are also frequently friends in the daytime as well. They are taught to cross access each other just as real siblings would be.

But at some point, they will be forced to hurt each other. If one "twin" is considered expendable, the ultimate set up will be one in which one twin is forced to die while the other watches. One twin may gather secrets from the other twin, be forced to disclose them to a trainer or cult leader then may be forced to kill the other. One twin may be forced to hit, or hurt the other. If they refuse, the trainer will brutalize the other twin, and the refusing twin told that the child was hurt because of their refusal to comply. Many setups will involve one twin being forced to betray the other, turning on the other child after intense programming. This betrayal set up will devastate both children, and they will learn the true lesson: trust no one. **Betray, or be betrayed.**

Internal structures: temples, eyes, mirrors, carousels etc. The Illuminati trainers will try to create internal structures within the person's personality systems. Why? They believe this creates better stability. It also gives the alters and fragments a place to "hang on to" inside, and creates a convenient way to call them up. If a fragment is indexed inside to an internal helix, for example, the trainer knows how to locate them more easily. Internal structures will vary greatly depending on the trainer, the group, the region of the U.S. or Europe and the goals for the individual. Common internal structures will include, but are not limited to:

Temples: these are often consecrated to principle Illuminati deities, and spiritual alters will congregate here. This may represent actual temples, Masonic or private that the subject may have visited.

Temple of Moloch will be created out of black stone with a fire burning internally.

All seeing eye of Horus: one of the most common structures in an Illuminati system; universal. Horus is a deity revered by the Illuminati, and the all seeing eye internally represents the fact that the cult can always see what the individual is doing. It will also represent being given to Horus in a high ceremony. The eye may be closed, or open, depending on the system's status at the time. This eye will also be linked to demonic watching of the person's activities at all time.

Pyramids: the Illuminati revere ancient Egyptian symbology, especially "mystery religion" and Temple of Set teachings. Pyramids will be placed internally both for stability (a triangle, and/or pyramid represents strength and stability), and as a calling place for the demonic. Pyramids and triangles, and the number three, represent calling up the demonic in Illuminist philosophy.

Sun: represents Ra, the sun god

Geometric figures: configurations of circles, triangles, pentagons, etc. Geometric patterns are considered sacred, and are based in ancient philosophy. There may be hundreds overlapping in a training grid for complex systems, which will house fragments in each one.

Training grids: these may be simplistic, such as cubes with patterns on them, rows of boxes, or more complex such as helixes, double helixes, infinity loops. Each trainer will have favorites classified as simple, medium and complex, depending on the child and its ability to recall and memorize.

Suicidal Programming is often the most dangerous programming that the survivor will face during their healing process. ALL ILLUMINATI SURVIVORS WILL HAVE SUICIDAL PROGRAMMING PROTECTING THEIR SYSTEMS. The Illuminati know and realize that with time, individuals in their group may start to question what they are doing. Or they may become disenchanted with their role. They may even desire to leave the group or try to dismantle their own programming. The trainers are well aware of this possibility and to prevent this, will always program in suicide. The suicide programming, may surround one or more systems internally. It may be layered into more than one system.

From earliest childhood, survivors have been conditioned to believe that they would rather die than leave their "family" (the Illuminati group). This is the core, or basis of suicidal programming. It will be closely linked to loyalty to one's family as well as the group (remember, this is a generational group and leaving it may mean giving up contact with one's parents, spouse, siblings, aunts, uncles, cousins and children, as well as close friends). These people will all try to contact the survivor, and try to draw them back into the cult, asking "don't you love us anymore?" or even becoming accusatory and hostile if the survivor does not respond the way they wish. The survivor will be told that they are "crazy" or delusional. That their family loves them and would never be part of a cult. The family members will all still be amnesic, unless something happens to trigger their own memories.

One of the most frequent suicidal programming sequences placed internally will be "come back or die " programming. A family member may activate it by telling the survivor that they are missed and their family wants to see them. If the survivor fails to return, the programming will start running. It can only be deactivated by a code word from the person's trainer or cult contact person. This ensures that they will recontact. If the survivor tries to break this programming, they will need assistance, both internal and external, for safety.

Chronometric suicidal programming is another type placed within. This does not need contact with family members to activate. In fact, it is activated automatically after a certain amount of time WITHOUT cult contact. Controller alters and/or punishing alters will have been programmed that if a certain period of time goes without contact with the trainer, they are to commit suicide. They will be told that the only way to prevent this is recontact with the trainer, who knows a command code to halt the program. The time interval may be anywhere from three months to nine months, each system is different.

Honor/dishonor programming is common in military systems. In this, the military parts are told that an "honorable and courageous" soldier will take his life, rather than reveal secrets or leave his unit.

Preventing Reaccessing of the Survivor
Deprogramming cannot be consistently successful if the person is still in contact with the abusers. Survivors will take one step forward, and then will find themselves knocked down internally. The cult has a vested interest in keeping its members. After all, it has spent generations telling its members that if they leave they will die, be killed, or go psychotic. It makes them quite unhappy to see someone who is quite alive and very

clearly not psychotic leave. It also makes their more restive members question the truth of what they have been told if they see someone get out.

Having a member leave may break the hold of some programming in other members. Trainers especially hate to see anyone leave, and grind their teeth over this problem at night. People leaving the cult are considered a training failure and the trainers may be punished severely.

So, the cult has come up with certain ways to keep their members with them, willingly or unwillingly. These include, but are not limited to: E.T. phone home (phone programming): the individual will have personalities whose sole job is to call and report to the trainer or cult leader. These are often young child alters who are eager to please, starved for attention and nurture, and who are heavily rewarded for calling back in. Any survivor who attempts to leave the cult must deal with the urge to phone home to phone their abusers. To phone their friends who are in the group. To phone their parents, siblings, cousins, or aunts. This urge may become overwhelming at times and worst of all, the survivor may be totally amnesic to the fact that the people they are calling are cult members who are urging them, in code, to come back.

Common phrases used include: your 'family' loves you, misses you, and needs you. So and so is ill and needs to see you. You are so special to us. You are so valuable. You need to come see us. Why are you so distant? Why haven't we heard from you lately? The list goes on and on. Sweet, kind phrases with double meanings, placed in the person during training sessions. Trainers are not stupid and know that if cult members said, "come to the ritual meeting at midnight next week", the survivor would run the other way, and be validated as well that they are not making things up. So, they ingrain code messages behind innocuous phrases such as described above. These, and other messages, are meant to trigger recontact programming.

ALL ILLUMINATI MEMBERS HAVE RECONTACT PROGRAMMING, IT IS NEVER LEFT TO CHANCE the person has parts whose only job is to have contact with their trainer or cult leader, or accountability person

(person one step above them in the cult). These parts are heavily programmed under drugs, hypnosis, shock, torture, to have recontact. The individual will feel restless, shaky, weepy, and afraid if they try to break this programming. It will often be linked or joined in to suicidal programming. They may experience PTSD symptomology, or even flood programming, and internal self-punishment sequences, as they fight this programming internally.

Siblings are often cross-trained to access each other with special codes. The survivor will need to go through a period of grieving for loss of contact with family members and friends in the cult. No matter how abusive, how disliked, it can be very difficult to cut off with perpetrators, especially if they were the only people close to the survivor. The survivor needs to acknowledge the difficulty of creating a new, healthy, cultless support group. The survivor needs to recognize that learning new skills and developing healthy friendships will take time.

Shell programming, Internal Councils, Human Experimentation, Function Codes

Your Entourage is Waiting for you to find them

a form of programming used to create a "shell" on the outside, that other alters inside speak through. This is a designed to hide the person's multiplicity from the outside world, and works extremely well with highly fragmented systems. It also takes a person with the ability to dissociate to a great degree. How it is done: with shell programming, the trainer will often take a clear plastic or glass mask, and put it in front of the subject. They will be extremely traumatized, shocked, drugged, and told that they (the alter or alters in front) are the "mask" that they see. Their job will be to be a shell, or voice, to cover for the others behind. These parts will be so traumatized that they literally see themselves as only a shell, with no real substance or body.

Others inside will then be directed to come next to the "shell" alters, and use their voice to cover their own. This allows greater fragmentation of the person, while being able to hide it from outside view, since the internal alters will learn to present through the shell. Shell alters always see themselves as "clear", and will have no color if color coding is present in other systems.

Internal Councils: Survivors of Illuminati programming will always have some type of hierarchy inside. This is because the cult itself is very hierarchical, and puts this hierarchy inside the person. What better way to inspire loyalty to leadership than to put the leadership inside the person's head? Trainers are also very hierarchy conscious themselves. They know that a system without hierarchy and head honchos inside to direct things will be a system in chaos. They will not leave the person's system leaderless inside.

PEOPLE TEND TO INTERNALIZE THEIR ABUSERS. The survivor may be horrified to find a representative of one of their worst perpetrators inside, but this was a survival mechanism. A tenet of human behavior is that often people will punish someone less who mimics them. A brutal Nazi will be less likely to punish another brutal Nazi, but will look down upon and punish a weak, crying person. So, the survivor will internalize the rough Nazi inside, to avoid being hurt.

Triads of three elders may be seen Platinum's may have a head council of three Jewels will have a triad, made up of ruby, emerald, diamond in many systems, to rule over the others an internal "leadership council", "System Above", "Ascended Masters", "supreme council", regional council, world council, etc. may be found. The councils found will vary with each survivor. It is not uncommon for the survivor to incorporate a parent, both parents, and grandparents, into their internal leadership hierarchy in a generational survivor.

High priests and priestesses may sit on ruling councils inside.

Human Experimentation The Illuminati were famed for deciding years ago to "go scientific" and incorporate scientific experimentation into their training principles. This is one area where they broke with other, more traditional groups, who still followed "spiritual principles". The Illuminati decided to use scientific data, especially in the psychiatric and behavioral sciences, to drive their training practices. This became known openly during W.W.II, when the world heard about the experimentation on Jews and other groups in the concentration camps, but human experimentation had been quietly going on for years before underground. It also did not stop at the end of the war. German trainers and scientists were scattered around the world, and hidden, where they continued teaching others the principles they had learned, and continued with ongoing experimentation. Some of this experimentation occurred with government funding through groups such as the CIA and NSA. The Illuminati had people infiltrated throughout these groups, who used the principles discovered and shared them with their own trainers.

Experimentation is going on, even to this day. It is done secretly. Its purpose is to help improve and create more sophisticated training techniques. To prevent "programming failures", or "pfs" as they are called in the cult.

Trainers like to tell their subjects that they are experiments, even if they aren't, for several reasons:

1. It creates immense fear and helplessness in the subject (the thought is, if this is an experiment, I will have to work really hard to survive this)

2. It devalues the person immensely. They will feel that they have no real value as a human being, that all they are is an experiment. Someone who feels devalued doesn't care, and will be willing to do things they wouldn't if they felt some value, some humanization.

3. It gives the trainer added power, as they are the one who can begin or stop the "experiment". Almost always, when the person is TOLD they are an experiment, it isn't really true. When trainers and cult members really do experiments, the subjects are never told, because it could bias results. The fear could interfere with drug effects, and skew the results. Most recent cult experimentation has been in the area of: drug effects: using different drugs, both alone and in new combinations and dosages, to induce trance states and open the person to training.

Effectiveness of new disks created to put programming in. Cult graphics and computer experts will work to create better and more effective VR disks, which are tested on cult subjects for their effectiveness. The cult wants more and more standardization, and less room for human error and weakness, in its training techniques, which is why it is going more and more to high tech equipment and videos.

Spiritual Programming Any discussion of Illuminati programming would be lacking if it did not address spiritual programming. Illuminati are first and foremost not scientists, but spiritual. The very foundation of the group is based on the occult. All children go to rituals, where they are dedicated from before birth as well as at intervals throughout their life. In these rituals, demonic entities are invoked, to coerce the person into servant hood, loyalty, and secrecy; as well as reinforce the programming being done.

Trainers will invoke demonic layering during programming sessions. This is done after acute trauma. The person is asked if they want more pain, and they will always say "no". The trainer then offers them a way out: if they will accept a "protector" or "protectors" they won't be hurt any more. The trainers will want this, knowing that with these "protectors'" they can shorten the training sessions. The protectors, or guardians, will reinforce the programming internally, without outside help. This concept will seem controversial to people who do not believe in spiritual realities, but I am only describing what the Illuminists believe, and their trainers practice.

Spiritual programming will also include: being forced to memorize rituals, THE BOOK OF ILLUMINATION, and other books which contain cult beliefs. The person will be saturated from infancy on, in classes and training sessions, with cult beliefs. They will go to rituals where the adults participate in spiritual worship, wearing robes, and giving obeisance to the group's particular guardian deity. Moloch, Ashtaroth, Baal, Enokkim are demons who are commonly worshipped. The child may see a sacrifice, either real or a set-up, to these deities; animal sacrifices are common. The child will be forced to participate in the sacrifices, and will have to go through blood baptism.

They will be forced to take the heart, or other internal organs, out of an animal that has been sacrificed, and eat them. The adults, and leaders of the group, will place their hands on the child's head, while it is drugged, and invoke demonic entities. One ritual, which is actually programming is the "resuscitation ritual". In this ritual, the child may be heavily drugged, and shocked or tortured, to the point that his heart may stop. The head priest will then "resuscitate " the child, using drugs, CPR, and incantations. When the child comes back, and is awake, he or she will be told that they were "brought back to life" by the demonic entity that the particular group worships, and that now the child owes it their life. They are told that if they ever tell, or try to get the demon to leave, they will return to the lifeless state they were in prior to resuscitation.

Spiritual "healings" due to the demonic are also common. Injuries caused by torture, or programming sessions, or even military exercises, will be healed almost instantaneously during invocations. Jewel programming will often have demons loyal to the generational family spirits layered in. These are called the "family jewels". The demons "guard them" and help protect the programming surrounding them.

Core splits, Denial programming, the last Five Steps of Discipline

Virtual Reality Programming (VR) is a form of programming that has become more and more widely used in the past few decades. It involves the person being placed in VR headsets and suit while a cult created VR disk is used to run the program. It can be used to create 3D and holographic images, and especially is useful in scripted programming, and target practice sequences for assassin training. Under hypnosis, the person will really believe they are in the scene.

Virtually any scenario can be recreated. Images to be "burned in" will be shown on the VR disk, and reinforced repetitively during the programming sequence. Some trainers feel it removes the element of "human error" in training, and use it quite extensively.

Denial Programming: begins with the first experiences the infant goes through in life. The child has been horrendously wounded and traumatized; yet the next morning, the adults around him are acting normally, as if nothing had happened. They are modeling a lifestyle of denial for the infant and young child. This is reinforced later by the child being told: "It was just a bad dream" (oh, how the child wants to believe this lie.

WOLF, BEAR, CROW programming

Another example of Satanic cults TWISTING meanings for their purpose of control and creating human robots was developed around 1977 in the northwest region of America. A take off of Medicine Cards that are used like tarot cards to discover your power through the ways of the animals.

All training in the northwest region of America is based on hunting modules and animal symbols. In "TRAINING" the small child is sexually assaulted and physically assaulted and forced to learn how to attack prey and use those practices of sexual and physical force all in perfect sequence and timing so your prey doesn't get free or doesn't tell or INFORM.

Your Entourage is Waiting for you to find them

BEAR—This is basic training provided to all males if they pass the original tests. The Bear training starts dividing your consciousness from your subconsciousness, making sure that what you learn is kept in the dark part of your mind or the unconscious. That will also force you to separate your daytime activity from your nighttime activity where your training takes place. In Bear training you learn the basics—to be aware in the woods, be aware of the enemy, and of all patterns and timing concerning attack but also keeping the TRAINING AND INFORMATION YOU LEARN in your unconscious.

You are attacked and pinned down and forced to play many games—of getting your prey, holding down your prey, and taking what you want from your prey. But in training you first have to BE the PREY.

MOUNTAIN LION—You ascend through many stages—Wolf, Bear, Crow—to reach the level of the mountain lion. Mountain Lions are known to **terrorize their prey** in surprise attacks. They encircle their prey, prance and are known for their intricate verbal calls to intimidate and scare their intended victim. Through their graceful movements, physical prowess and specialized aptitude for killing their prey, they can make easy and very CLEAN kills. The small children are trained to be leaders. They will be attacked and terrorized to the point of near death by other "Mountain Lion" level children to make sure they understand the FEAR AND WEAKNESS of the prey.

That fear in the prey is what drives you to succeed and you lead others below you and in your group by utilizing that **fear** ALONG with your skills of **surprise attack** and **physical terrorization**. You can climb great distances and observe your prey and report back to your "Cave", your "Clan". The child is shown many films and tested about the mountain lion and how it attacks. In training they hunt and kill many mountain lions. The child CLIMBS showing AGILITY, OBSERVES PREY, instills FEAR, TERRORIZE, SURPRISE ATTACK.

The child works alone as a mountain lion but always NEEDS to report back to the clan, which they lead. In order to keep everyone happy you have to **LIE TO THEM**. That is the key to leadership. As "prince

Your Entourage is Waiting for you to find them

of the lions", you can demand and take whatever you choose from anyone who is in your clan—sex, money, power.

LIGER—Created by mating a trained Tigress with a trained Lion, the liger is a genetic hand-me-down of the Lion Clan. The ligers are not active if the subject does not cooperate with training, they will be used as a "liger"—a genetic showpiece much like the original animal liger.

This child is subjected to many programming experiments because of their status as being a HALF-BREED between two powerful higher hierarchies—the Tiger and the Lion. Those experiments range from genetics to get you to look as good as possible so people will want you and you will be sold for your uniqueness as a "liger". You are merely a showpiece, a face, and a body and will be used and abused as such. Ligers, like the animal liger, due to the experimentation and abuse, do not have long life spans. They most likely do not live past the age of 30-35. The Liger is understood throughout the Clan as a failed trainee of the Lion Clan. You will be abused, degraded and used until your humiliation from the sexual and physical abuse along with the genetic and programming experimentation ends in your death.

Chapter 4
COSMIC FLOW

When you RESIST the voice of your heart or entourage that sounds like you WITHIN you, YOU are resisting your invisible 90%er and **not the devil**. In your entourage you will notice some dark aspects that are there to give you contrast. Contrast is our gift to better understand THE LIGHT. Use your DISCERNMENT to decide if you want to follow the light or dark bits of your entourage. We chose to live on this planet of free will.

The COSMIC INTELLIGENCE or energy knows where it's going and what it's going to do and whom it will affect. Cosmic intelligence shines on humans to light the way for them and increase their clarity. Cosmic intelligence allows the human free choice and healing if that is their awareness and choice. The cosmic flow is not a source of sickness but you have **the option to resist wellness**. We are divine and we create your own universe when we are balanced and can create harmony in our universe. When humans are challenged, they rise to the occasion. Much of what we are creating will be new environments made from the rubble of old ones and how do you live in peace with the other divinity?

The collective vibration becomes an entity in the same way you make a corporation a legal entity. You will start to understand where real, healthy competition is, where you spur people on instead of trying to out do or beat them at something. All collective vibrations will now be successful if they can make space for the empowered human that all humans are becoming.

In trying to understand human behavior, I haven't found any magic. I have always found behavior to be pretty logical having PERDICTABLE causes and effects. The same treatment of an infant or adult most always results in the same kinds of behavior. Understanding cause and effect can help people understand what happened in their life and when things started to get a bit twisted. Then they have the power to alter it if they want to.

Your Entourage is Waiting for you to find them

When there are behaviors that don't seem to make sense, it is because you haven't discovered all that has happened to the individual. For example, when your vehicle needs fixing, the mechanic will ask what the car was doing "out of the ordinary" before you brought it in so he knows where to look for the trouble. When you know what an individual was doing before he or she got into trouble you can know what area needs to be serviced.

One process for **understanding** cause and effect:

1. Observe what is thought, said, and done so you can evaluate whether the effect makes sense and is desirable.
2. When the effect is not desirable, change the underlying belief, thought, or behavior by considering other options and picking a viable one or two.
3. Implement what changes you can and evaluate the results of those changes.
4. Repeat the process as often as necessary until the desired effect has been achieved. Observing, altering, adjusting, and getting improved results is a lifelong

process. Ideally, acquiring the tools for doing that should start in infancy.

There is a need to TRAIN THE EMOTIONS to be positive.

Emotion is just another word for **VIBRATION.** When the 10%er decides to be out of sync with the love, well being and compassion the legion of light continuously sends that human IS probably UNCONSCIOUS and unaware of their 90%er and the flow. That human is feeling negative and unhappy. Some humans wonder why GOD hates them. GOD or the "legion of light" wonders why the human is not in the cosmic flow. The human does not remember that they are 100% RESPONSIBLE for their own joy. Not the legion of light or your mom, or any angel in the unseen world is responsible for your joy, only YOU are responsible. Your balance and alignment can be found working with your entourage or soul. Reach and feel, reach and feel for the feeling of your soul. Your ENTOURAGE is WAITING for you to find them. With the variety of experiences found on Gaia we develop new preferences and broadcast the wanting of them to the unseen world, which in turn creates synchronicities for the human.

We are being called back to OUR-SELVES and when we are aware of that we can start opening up to experiencing life as SIMPLE and easy, **beautiful** and *rewarding*. Ultimately a souled being cannot get lost. We can pretend to be lost or forget we are only having an experience. BUT there is always the voice or the signs that call you back to yourself. That is what we are experiencing on earth at this time. Struggling is not needed and is very old energy.

For things to be easy and beautiful we DO NEED to be **present in our lives** someone needs **"to be home"** in your body. It is not possible to be the creator of your life when you have vacated your biology. Without acknowledging our self nothing can come to be or created other than the appearance of chaos, destiny and others choosing on your behalf. Humans abandon their biology because they **HURT** in the third dimension. Now we get to the good news. **You can** and should control all aspects of YOU.

Most of humanity is CONTROLLED by one bully or another and do not even try to take their power back. Their created REALITY is pain and suffering by surrendering to the bully. The legion of light is filled with unity and compassion. **Not filled with rules.** It is beautiful and filled with songs. Everyone is on very different paths and at different points on their path.

The old ways of creating and dealing with life just aren't available any longer for those moving into the new energy and oneness with their soul. The old ways do not want us to try and resurrect them either. *Old ways have left the building and your life.* We are working to create a variety of new solutions at this time. Those old tools aren't working like they used to work and in many cases they are just no longer available or working.

A friend was telling me when they were stressed they ate to calm themselves and they would dissociate for a bit or leave their body. But lately that is not working for him any longer. The stuffing of food didn't calm or enable a temporary escape as it always had done previously. Yes I agree, that is a very sad story.

Another friend was trained as a child that he "HAD TO DO" this and that to please all the adults in her life. This training created a "pleasing," very stressed child and adult with many addictions to overcome. With the advent of the crystalline energy she has released her "Have to do list" for others. Now she is doing only her "Have to do list" now.

Selfish is good as that is the only one you CAN please the SELF. We are no longer in service to others and that game is so over. Hear the crowd cheering! If you haven't already done it THE time is NOW to **UNCHOOSE** being in service to others. That would include in service to THE SOURCE our **angelic families** and all the other humans. CONSCIOUSNESS is awareness from every part of you including your stomach, shoulders, back and ALL of your SENSES and mind, your dreams and your imagination. Have awareness of your external environment, other people and your entourage.

Our emotional reactions to our experiences in life send out a vibration to the universe and that is how we create OUR own PERSONAL reality. That is how we create our own world. Each person on this planet is in charge of creating their own personal world and **no one else's**. Our emotion tells the law of attraction this is what I want more of. What you give your attention to invites more of the same to come into your life. The universe does not know about or care about **human ACTION** or words only your vibration. Even our animals and pets and sometimes our children do not trust or believe our words. You are creating what you want consciously or unconsciously it is always your choice. The universe does not know about or care whether your emotion is a result of the way you are LIVING or what you are **imagining**.

Your emotions and NOT YOUR WORDS **are tied to your feeling.** There is no value in using positive words when you do not FEEL the way you are talking. Your dominant emotion or feeling is where you vibrate at and that becomes your point of attraction to the universe. It is all a multidimensional math problem for the universe to decide what you are ready for. They do not want the human to miscreate and put themselves in overwhelm.

THOUGHT has no wavelength, no space and no time impinging on it in our physical universe which **DOES HAVE** space, time, energy and physical matter TO DEAL WITH. Thought is the perception of the present, compared to the past so one can draw conclusions for direct action in the now. **Thought controls ENERGY.** It is thought that causes everything structural and functional that happens. Thought ALWAYS comes FIRST experience is second. Our thoughts control our world and us. Are you being responsible for your THOUGHTS and **actions?** Without **focus** and GROUNDING you can loose your ENERGY or momentum.

Invisible realm is not here to help HUMANS STAY on their PATH. Oh but they have many answers and synchronicities for us. It is how we handle our self and the events in our life that LIMIT or ALLOW us to excel and grow. Learn to place yourself in environments where you feel good and do well. The THIRD DIMENSION is a holographic illusion created by our thoughts and perceptions that are essential parts of this reality we perceive. The nature of our reality is dictated by the energy of light and sound frequencies existing in our holographic field. We are now receiving vast infusions of cosmic light particles and harmonic vibrations from the legion of light.

So we can **perceive reality** in a new way we are creating a new holograph on the collective consciousness. Earth has been a low vibrational planet and we have put a **higher vibrational planet** hologram over it. The elements on the earth not vibrating high enough will have difficulty holding together and most of the time the lower vibrating entity will FALL APART or leave this planet. You must gain control over your thoughts.

People do not realize that they can be in charge of their own minds. **The more intensely focused you are the faster your energy moves. Thoughts and emotions are interwoven.** All thoughts no matter how boring carry some emotional reaction even if it is subtle. Emotion is a pleasant or unpleasant mental state organized in the limbic system of the mammalian brain. Like aromas, emotions are experienced, as positive or negative, pleasant or unpleasant emotions do not seem to be neutral. **Humans ARE able to direct their thoughts** and consequently their emotions or are the emotions directing your thoughts. We can see things as they REALLY are and we are VERY capable of **imagining things the way we would like them to be** and sustain that thought. Discern when ANYTHING is too overwhelming, horrendous or negative for you to experience and **LEAVE it.** When your reactions are very practiced it is harder for you to redirect them. Like the thoughts and beliefs our family, church or country have handed down to us as law and absolute truths. All that control and judgment are tricky to move in another direction or release. We need to be in control of our EMOTIONS and THOUGHTS so we can flow through life without hurting others. First and foremost learn not to hurt yourselves. Instead of mentally looping on thoughts of worry, shame, blame and guilt replace them with happier thoughts.

We exist and were created to **use and FLOW energy.** The connection and communication between soul and the human happens all day every day. In spite of the human feeling isolated and alone so much of the time the connection and communication is always there. We can own it or deny it. When you deny or block your feelings you do not know "How it is" with the rest of your 90%er. When you are feeling the opposite of YOUR legion of light you feel disempowered and THE VICTIM in bondage having NEGATIVE OR NO EMOTION or being UNCONSCIOUS you feel resentful and antagonistic or you blame when you are not in alignment with the rest of you.

The way to raise your vibration is to STAY IN YOUR BODY be very aware of yourself and focus on the pleasant higher thoughts at the level just above where you are at emotionally now. **Your emotions** and NOT YOUR WORDS **are tied to your feeling.** There is no value in using positive words when you do not FEEL the way you are talking. Your dominant emotion or feeling is where you vibrate at and that becomes your point of attraction to the universe. Even if it is all in your imagination it is all-good. The negativity we keep becomes a handicap and many do not know how to replace that negativity with a more positive outlook and TO CHANGE THE NEGATIVITY means going up against the family traditions. The family wants you to stay PUT. The invisible realm says that 90% of humans are depressed to one degree or another and it is getting worse as the planet is vibrating higher and those in negative emotional states are trapped even more than before. We certainly were never encouraged to imagine our way out of depression with positive thoughts. Unless my mother telling me, "If you had storm windows and screens to put on and take off you wouldn't have time to be depressed." Is a way to imagine your self out of depression? Certainly that never worked to make me more joyful. We maintain our negative beliefs out of ignorance and not realizing how detrimental they are to us. We never thought negative beliefs would hurt us.

My father defined himself as living in the "land of negativity." Many times he stated that the world was out to get him. He owned NO responsibility for the pain and suffering he perpetrated on the children he traumatized. After all look at all the generations back that behaved that way and they did JUST FINE with their negative beliefs. Didn't they? If it does not feel good AVOID IT or focus **ONLY on the good parts.** You create reality by **GIVING IT YOUR attention** and **feeling**. Everything about the universe **IS spiritual**. Practice living the way you would like to live. The universe doesn't know or care if you are emoting in response to something you are LIVING or IMAGINING. Regurgitating or reinforcing what you want often and you start accepting it as reality. That is creating your reality. NO ONE **NEEDS you** to be or DO anything in order to be fulfilled

OUR JOURNEY back to SELF. The thoughts we give **focus** and **attention** to
LITERALLY create the journey we are on.

Our thoughts FILTERED through our attitudes and beliefs trigger an emotional reaction. Thoughts + BELIEF'S + emotions = the sum of our identity. Who and what we think we are. As we think, we are identifying a cluster of energetic pulses that have associated themselves with a concept matching your energy and enhancing your packet of THOUGHT through an electrical charge, which **magnetizes it** to attract more of the same.

YOUR life requires YOUR attention and creative energy. FOCUS on YOU. Draw the energy into YOU from YOUR entourage. The energetic cluster or thought, promotes a belief in itself as reality and WHEN you align with it you create a truth for you. Then you own it and take possession of the thought. You identify yourself with that thought and what it means. You start to function within the framework of your thoughts.

The choices of thoughts you align with become YOUR VERSION of reality.

Travel INSIDE the SELF to **gain control of your THOUGHTS.** Redirect your negative THOUGHTS. In the NOW moment excitement, stimulation and beauty are easily perceived. A different set of synapses FIRE in the brain when you complain or blaming. The more negativity you dwell in the deeper the ditch you dig gets. Give attention to and hear the words out of your mouth. We are striving and seeking to understand love within everything we say and do. When you see and judge something as ugly that is YOUR FOCUS and judgment just like the perfect flower or person is. The human experience is one of the most difficult experiences for soul in the universe. And now the human electromagnetic field (EMF) is being stretched and pulled by the increasing energies of our planet to operate in the quantum crystalline field that is here and the human aura is being transformed into the high vibration of the crystalline field.

A LAW in the PHYSICAL UNIVERSE

There is a law in the PHYSICAL universe that never changes.

PERCEPTION produces reality. Physical reality magnifies your perception into the visible. Visible reality through our senses reproduces itself over and over again creating a stronger belief and more concrete reality. **Belief** produces **emotion** and emotion strengthens our belief. Everything we experience is from the highest understanding we personally have of our level of truth. We see our "point of perception" and call it reality. On earth we have many DIFFERENT personal realities. At this time our thought can be replaced by our soul's thought or spiritual reality and then we can experience the material universe for the illusion it really is.

The crystalline energy and grid system is clearing and clarifying the view for us to elevate our thoughts. Money, drama and drugs are sedatives to avoid feeling WHAT you really feel. Invisible realm can teach balance, structure and setting good solid boundaries so you can have **respect and love for yourself**. With the new bias of light on earth since 1987 every child born is getting an indigo imprint or vibration. The magnetic grid of the planet does that. Millions of children are growing up with a different consciousness than those 28 years and older have. The new Indigos do disagree amongst them selves about the best way to bring compassion to earth. New cultural attributes must be developed and learned.

Indigo's even have a different type of duality than we had. They are not struggling to survive as we did the Indigo's want **more enjoyment** and TIME to enjoy. Their integrity and ethics are in place. They are not in a hurry to gather STUFF around them and amass wealth like we were. Leaders are getting elected because of their compassion for those around them, and their good ideas for those around them, not just because they're popular or charismatic. They are very supportive of each other rules are changing in all areas and fields. We are deciding minute by minute what we want. We are experiencing an economic pruning, renaissance or restructuring in finance and other areas.

COMMON SENSE is our idea of what works naturally in a given level of awareness. When YOUR consciousness changes SO **does your common sense**. For example consider what has changed in the last twenty years. Did your common sense predict that? Consider how our conversations have changed and what we find interesting to talk about. Our common sense has changed and our goals and values have changed. Historically we have used visualization of what we want and took the appropriate steps to get there. That is not the best way to go now. The best results and outcomes come from aligning with the synchronicity that the invisible realm puts together for our awareness. Young people are fleeing from membership in the churches. The doctrines are too ridged and do not make sense to them. Organized religion can thrive with a core that has far more INTEGRITY than it has ever had historically.

WE are not going to beat terrorism with terrorism. We are not going to beat an old energy FORCE with **force**. THAT does not work. It's perpetually a failure. The more terrorism fails to work, the less there will be. Terrorism will create disgust even among those who used to feel it was the only way. Ideas that create harmony and balance will attract converts and the young. Tolerance will be the way of things, as the young people become the leaders. They know violence does not create peace. Violence, abuse and control create sadness and depressed robots.

DEATH from a human point of perception feels a little like slipping into a pool of warm water. There is a moment of SURRENDER when we move from one environment and point of perception into another. Your awareness does not actually go anywhere but you are no longer in biology. Death is a cessation of your biology. Life, awareness and personality go on. You experience a more expanded version of HERE than you experienced as a human. The expanded version has been present all along but you did not perceive it. The expanded version will not seem physical or non-physical but a bit lighter in density or buoyant as we feel our biology in salt water. It is best to focus and be alert at this point of separation from your biology because what you experience is what YOUR thoughts have created and that will become your environment as you enter your new reality. The calmer you are the more direction you have and the less confused you get.

We will not feel temperature as we did in the third dimension because it was our biology that felt warm or cold. Our point of arrival is a temporary place and when it has served its purpose it will begin to dissolve and a more appropriate place will appear. We feel more like our self on the other side and comfortably connected to others. You will feel more a part of the web of life than you do now. You have a body but it will not necessarily look like a human body. It will be more translucent, and seem to you that you are dressed in light, or a light-like substance.

80% of those that die get lost in the forth dimension frequently and start the cycle of taking a body and going back to the forth dimension and ultimately staying earth bound. Of those that keep cycling from a body to forth dimension only ten percent are able to evolve out of that and get to the bridge of flowers on there own. At death humans have a type of conditioning that reminds us instantly of the many, many times we have crossed over before. We have crossed over thousand or more times so we know the drill. The consciousness of crossing over comes back shortly before death actually and helps us release our biology easier.

The human biology is primarily a vehicle for the 10% of your soul that wants to live in and experience matter. The soul is drawn to the vehicle that is most appropriate for what it wants to accomplish.

The biggest issue is that most humans cannot decide if they want to be here or elsewhere. We must connect to our invisible parts so that when you're headed down the road of negative thinking you can stop and redirect yourself. Those negative thoughts get caught in the spiritual, mental, emotional and physical body processes. If you can get to the mental world first when you're having a bad day, hour or minute, you will be able to turn it around into this new force of light that is guided by your higher selves. During the shifting process, the percentage of your brain that is active will open up more and more.

Opening up your PERCEPTIONS opens up to the path of ascension. To move to a higher realm and leave the incarnation cycle you might need assistance. This journey is about our THOUGHTS and raising them to a higher level of awareness.

Human's biologies are really luminous balls of light. The physical form that you see now in the third dimensional is an assumed body that represents many energy aspects of the person, including past lives, illnesses, densities and the effects of experiences in the third-dimensional life. You would be able to see the true energetic pattern of the person you see. If you were able to experience higher light and then have a corresponding opening in your perceptual field, then you would be able to experience people as energetic luminous balls of light. The energy patterns that make up your third-dimensional body are at such a high frequency that your normal perceptual ranges and training don't allow you to see all levels of your luminous body. And in fact, if you did see the luminous energy balls now then you could become confused and you wouldn't know what to make of it. In the ascension only some people are going to have the ability to participate fully in the increase in light. The codes of ascension are in your DNA codes and in certain parts of your brain, which are dormant. It needs to be awakened, but it cannot be awakened unless there is a proper preparation and unless there is the proper circuitry established to hold higher vibrational frequency. The **vibrational frequency of ascension is a higher than normal energy.** Certain higher energies with exercises were given to the mystics.

    Having a LIGHT BODY means you are energetically lighter because you released INTERNAL pockets of your density. ARTHRITIS is crystallized anger in the joints, creating joint blockages in the nervous system meridian flows. The energetic baggage and negativity human's carry keep them heavy and dense. HEART issues and palpitations are the body's rhythmic adjustments to the increasing frequencies. SUGAR imbalances, is too much unhappiness in life leading to an inability to process the sweet. When you heal the wounds that occurred during your lifetime you are healing the residue of what you are not.

The wounds that have occurred are events that have supported the illusion of separation. We have set up life so releasing these wounds takes great effort and energy. We respond to wounding events with EMOTION that result in a chemical response creating an imprint of pain in our cells and our neurons. That makes it difficult to totally release the event and pain that caused the wound. When you are vibrating high enough your entourage brings the cosmic flow of energy through you so you experience the oneness. When you are seeing something that you judge to be negative or ugly, you are in separation from your invisible parts. When you judge something or one as negative or ugly you are judging an aspect of your self. What you judge as ugly is actually an illusion. Stay in your heart and stop judgment, blame and gossip. Holding on to truths of yesterday puts us backs in pastime and we bring the past forward to make it our future.

PEACE

Peace is the ability to allow everything and everyone to be exactly as they are. Within real peace there is *no need to be right* or have a **right way** to be peaceful. The seeds of peace are a potential creation waiting to match the human vibration of peace. Little humans envision peace as everyone satisfied with no hunger or pain. On a planet of **free choice** that is NOT POSSIBLE. There is **one Earth** as there is one you. We remake ourselves continuously in creative and endless expressions. All of our expressions are still of us. TRUST in your infinite ability to remake you and your experiences.

We can be free of **MAJOR wars**.

One world government won't work. Humans need **different LEADERS** and governments to maintain profoundly ***different ways of life***. Governments and communities will intertwine in very unique ways. Peace needs to be made of agreements to respect each other's choice of HOW they want to live and exist. No more ***forcing others*** from family members to countries. There will always be disputes, hunger and situations where many need what others have. Neighbors will trade with neighbors. Neighbors will need and depend on each other.

That will be the way of peace. The earth is crowded and full of people and places this is not a simple time. ALL need to give to receive the abundance of the earth and its humans in the **WAY it is offered. RECEIVE** abundance in the MANNER it is OFFERED. **DO** not claim more than you NEED. Earth can house the cold, feed the hungry and drive away thirst and petty tyrants will not control it any longer. Arm yourselves against danger and protect the home of the soul or all will be lost. Earth and her resources are on LOAN. The wealth of Gaia will redistribute itself fairly as humanity needs to do. We left our "homes" eons ago on a mission we volunteered to help each world we entered. Agreeing to adopt their lifestyle and ways. We teach the ways of the legion of light.

ROMANTIC HUMAN RELATIONSHIP

Conditional love is a unique human invention and has worked well enough in the lower vibrations. Old energy romantic relationship certainly can be updated and brought into the new energy if both parties want that and would enjoy that. Many of our old energy relationships ended because the contract between the humans no longer served them. In the new energy the old contracts of security and "till death does us apart" have lost their meaning and usefulness. In old energy many were attached to the idea or concept of HAVING a RELATIONSHIP and NOT the concept of the relationship based on love from the heart for each other. As humans evolve they **release attachment** to the concept of conditional love and move to UNCONDITIONAL love.

As we vibrate higher we move into unconditional multidimensional love. When you have melded with your soul finding a romantic relationship is a job best left up to the SOUL and not the human. Soul does the creating of synchronicities and hooks you up! The number of partners and your sexual preference is ALSO the souls choice. The soul listens to and honors the little humans input and preferences. But soul knows a LOT more than the human does about what the human would enjoy the most. Your soul can find and choose a higher vibrational love for you. Find you a SOVEREIGN human that will bond with you in STRONG friendship and CONSTRUCTIVE purpose on multidimensional levels. At home, work or daily living they will have **excellent COMMUNICATION**. They are **conscious** and AWARE of all their energies and all the energies around them. Higher vibrational love and romance understands what goes on around them. They understand what is said and needed. They share SIMILAR values and vibrations.

Members feel free to speak their mind to the other human(s) and that makes the relationship thrive. This is deep heartfelt communication and understanding. This is not tolerating someone because of their money or good looks or they are a bully. With deeper levels of communication and understanding you get heightened sexual experiences. The purpose of sex in the higher vibrations is to express UNCONDITIONAL love, which allows us the highest benefit from sexual activity physically, emotionally, mentally and spiritually.

LOVE HOLOGRAMS

It is not possible to make a hologram with CONDITIONAL love because that is linear and single dimensional. With multidimensional, unconditional love you can build a love hologram to support your relationship. Focus on the way another makes you feel. Then find another point to fall in love with. Consider another aspect of them that you love. Think of each aspect as a beam of light hitting the same heart from different angles. Like many points of perception focused on one spot or object. SOME EXAMPLES of beams of light: When someone shares their insides with you, Honesty and bringing information to share, Open and available for truthful interaction, Gives 100% of your focus when interacting, Kind and generous nature Wears flowers. Put all these points of perception together in the ethers and you have a love hologram energy imprint that stays in the ethers. When the hologram is left, without interference, energy will naturally gather around it.

You can create a love hologram to enhance another thing you like including business, projects and many levels of relationships. All of it is based on unconditional love. A love hologram greatly affects communication in a positive way when there is high regard for each side. Having a high regard allows you to see yourself in a very unique way.

The LIGHTER side of life *keeps energy flowing* and leads you into **FULL MEMORY and recall** of yourself. Humor, laughter, lightness are all key ingredients to remembering.

CHANGE CONTINUES.

Are you venting and lashing out against the changes going on in the FLOW and the many different realities on earth now?

Your Entourage is Waiting for you to find them

Are you allowing your fear to run your life? Those clinging to traditional beliefs and being guided by fear and guilt feel anxious and confused. The other group, are the ones seeking **enlightenment** and AWARENESS and feel that things are finally moving in a LOVING, **supportive** direction. They are feeling *positive and hopeful.* Our lessons are leaving and we are having the opportunity to become divine humans **AFTER we have met some basic requirements.** Like controling your THOUGHTS and BELIEFS.

    The little human needs to give up control to your soul or entourage. We are 100% soul taking 10% of the soul to have a human experience by turning into MATTER to gaining *spiritual wisdom* for the soul. When our perceptions are altered and our values and truths have changed we have probably changed levels. Each level of vibration carries a ratio of Light to **DARK** commensurate with the way the little human thinks and feels. These levels of dark and light vibration move within a range. The smaller the percentage of light the human has, the smaller their ability is to be flexible and compassionate. To vibrate high enough for your soul to reach the lower vibration of the human we need control over our little human thoughts and emotions.

The little human needs to: Discontinue its **NEGATIVITY** and terminate **JUDGING the self.** End GOSSIP and complaining it is not useful drama. Know you have all you **need** there is **NO lack**. Focusing on things **NOT wanted** lowers your vibration and ability to create and be compassionate. Higher or lower vibrations are placed by the degree of HARMONY or *discord present* in them. Those humans having less than 60% light are **too dense** to feel love and compassion from the invisible realm. **The nature of our angelic reality is BASED in thought.**

Chapter 5
3rd, 4th and 5th DIMENSION

Each dimension is shaped like a sphere or huge ball. All the spheres INTERACT with each other. DIMENSIONS are *ONLY CONSCIOUSNESS* and do NOT occupy any **time or ANY space.** You can create as many dimensions as would please you there are "no limits" and dimensions are exceedingly *flexible*. Dimensions swirl, move, shift and intersect each other all the time. There are positive and negative dimensions and unpredictable dimensions. Sometimes they are identical to each other before they split off and go on their own to become different dimensions not on a mental level but on a multidimensional KNOWINGNESS level.

Dimensions contain elements of each other and have a THEME or purpose. For example all the different ways to build a harp would be on one dimension. All the thoughts that have ever been thought about a given subject, for example "building solar houses" or "doing division" will all be in one separate dimension. When you commune with the invisible realm or other dimensions you can go to that dimension and collect information BUT you NEED to **discern** what information will serve your needs best as the helpful and not so helpful thoughts will all be there together. Each dimension has a *certain vibration* that is fixed. The dimension on "how to torment living things" would be a slow vibration and rather negative.

The universe exists in many DIMENSIONS all at once. Dimensions are defined by their **WAVELENGTH** or FREQUENCY. Time and space are constant in the third dimension but do not exist in other dimensions. A human has several concurrent or happening all at one time dimensions of realities. There are many versions of us existing side by side in slightly different dimensional realities. When we solve problems or do certain spiritual things we GO interdimensional in the process. The most interdimensional thing we have is our own DNA. Working with your **past** or parallel **lives** in any form is working with interdimensional energy. Creator thoughts and idea's shoot from this dimension into other dimensions and return BACK to their creator CHANGED. ***Expansional*** energy always finds its way back to you the zero point in PRESENT TIME.

We travel in space by going into one dimension and out into another. Traveling in SPACE is a matter of shifting dimensions. Shifting our thoughts and energy moves and flows our awareness in and out of dimensions. We solve challenges by going through the dimensions to collect needed information. One of the great uses of crystalline energy is to travel on it between dimensions. It is a matter of using and expressing the energy anyway you please.

Dimensions are POCKETS of ENERGY MOVEMENT and not levels. We each move along in our own pocket of energy. Scientists say there are at least eleven dimensions in the heart of atomic structure but they forgot to count the dimension zero. Dimensional parallel planes are often holographic in nature and can exist devoid of space. They are not truly places but a parallel holographic plane may be inserted into a specific time as a mental reality. It can be a specific stand-alone reality that is capable of existing separately, but this does not lessen its validity by any means. On a macrocosmic level dimensions are nothing more than light breaking through a prism.

We can rise through the dimensions by melding into higher or lower frequencies. Higher frequency THOUGHTS will correct IMBALANCES of dense lower pockets of energy.

THIRD DIMENSION

The 3rd dimension is a holographic illusion created and SUSTAINED with our thoughts and perceptions of this reality and how we perceive it. The nature of our reality is dictated by the energy of light and sound frequencies existing in our holographic field and thoughts.

The legion of light has sent vast infusions of cosmic light particles to earth since 1987. Vibrating at a higher vibration to bring the entire planet UP in vibration through the 4th and into the 5th dimension. They have penetrated the existing third dimensional fields and are creating new holographic fields so that the collective consciousness can **perceive** a new reality. When the planet was very dense our perception was limited to a narrow linear pattern. The new patterns support wholeness and a sense of wellbeing in humans, animals and plants. SUFFERING is **self-perpetuating**, and is supported ONLY when you ALLOW victimhood, being a predator or a silent watcher as we have been doing in the 3rd dimension. We decided other human's THOUGHT and beliefs were more powerful than our own.

  The third and fourth dimension darkness of Draco's and the largest negative group is the dark Orion's, formerly the Lords of Rigel, reptilians and various other factions do not have a vibration sufficient to remain on earth after approximately 2030. Most will be gone after 2012 they will be unable to possess their subjects and will depart the earth for other regions of the galaxy. They took over this planet approximately five hundred thousand years ago by acquiring our natural resources and hording them. As a result we find more wars about petroleum products and fresh drinking water occurring. They work hard to make us fearful so they can feed on our energy of fear.

THIRD to FOURTH dimensions have duality, negative and positive emotions. Both have spiritual and mental bodies, only the third dimension has BIOLOGY. Currently earth is moving from the third dimension to the fourth dimension and on to the fifth dimension.

The nature of SOUND and LIGHT are more vibrant and powerful now. There is an increase of light on earth and the sun and moon are whiter than they ever have been. Only those with a higher light frequency are able to use it because their awareness will increase. They will be able to see the connections we have to other beings of light. The "etheric cords" or "strands of light." These etheric cords or strands are on everyone. However, some people's etheric cords or strands only go into the third dimension. Your etheric strands of light are connected to the fifth dimension now because you have been working with us. With the connection of the etheric strands of light, during the ascension process you will be able to project and have your luminous body move to where those etheric cords are attached namely the fifth dimension. When you move the etheric body then the luminous body follows it. I make a distinction between the luminous body and the etheric body. The physical body is an energy field.

LIGHT is a powerful energy and **spans** all DIMENSIONAL LEVELS **simultaneously.** The true vibration of light will rejuvenate our biology and soul. The higher meaning of Light is enlightenment or spiritual wisdom. Light can be reflected and that is easier for us to do instead of being the Light. GRACE mimics the natural FLOW of Light. Humans have earned the right to walk fully in the grace of the divine. When the word light hits your ears a resonance starts up creating an **interdimensional** vibration that weaves dimensions together to ACT AS ONE.

Darkness can do nothing to affect light, but light can destroy darkness. The most divine place on earth, with the most Light on this planet, exists in the human mind. There's no group of bright, white angels who are standing by to take your hand and whip you into heaven should you choose to go. Instead they're standing by in full regalia, willing to celebrate and love and press upon you with their energies to let you know they're there.

Light is the only one of dark and light that has an active component and a physical presence. You cannot "beam" darkness into a light place! It can only be the other way around. If you have a dark place and light comes in darkness does not creep away into another dark place. Instead, it's transformed! Put your hand on a wall, your hand stops because you experience the wall as solid. If you are in a higher perceptual field, then you can see the wall is an energetic field. When you experience states of higher consciousness you can actually put your hand through the wall.

The physical body follows the luminous body. You, who are Arcturian star seeds, came to the Earth in your luminous ball of light with many star seed luminous strands. To enter into the fifth world you must open your heart and follow the sacred path. Remember who you are, where you came from and where you are going. "Let there be Light." Our concept of light needs expansion light is a visceral experience a feeling experience. Light encompasses everything. Light is the source of all creation.

FOURTH DIMENSION

The 4th dimension is more of a transitory space for humans, all living things and Gaia to adjust to the new higher frequencies gradually. YOUR higher AWARENESS fuels the fourth dimension. The higher your consciousness is the stronger your BRIDGE is between the third and fifth dimensions. Our consciousness and creations happen faster in the fourth dimension than they do in 3rd dimension. After our biology dies and we are STILL in the astral realm and the earth's incarnation cycle we will be reborn again in the third dimension and have a new biology. In certain situations having a low vibration at you death might get you reborn in an appropriate energy field on another planet. Staying in the fourth dimension realms after your death means you remain in the third dimensional incarnation cycle. THIRD to FOURTH dimensions have duality, negative and positive emotions. You can divide the forth dimension into three parts.

LOWER ASTRAL plane of 4th DIMENSION

The fourth dimension has lower layers you might NOT want to stay in. They are filled with the earthbound, the lost gray ones, the addicted, ghosts and spirits. A dark place filled with HOPLESSNESS. These levels seem to be places of PUNISHMENT because entities feel stuck in a chain of limiting, dark, low vibrational beliefs that are REPETITIOUS. They are trapped in an illusion of darkness they feel unable to evolve out of. They have little chance to gather more light and wisdom because there are not many resources available in the forth dimension like there is in the third dimension.

Nothing is eternal on the lower astral realm even though it might FEEL like it will last forever. Lower astral beings can and do suck energies from 3rd dimensional beings on earth. The only means of escape for entities without biologies SEEMS to be parasitic attachment to earth biology. These lower beings that have attached to people contribute to their doing some pretty nasty things.

MIDDLE ASTRAL plane of 4th DIMENSION

The middle astral layer on the other hand, is a higher energy and there are some very high beings there.

HIGHER ASTRAL plane of 4th DIMENSION

The higher fourth dimensional astral realm is beautiful and is getting close to the fifth dimension. There are many guides and teachers there and new energies that are reshaping the world.

FIFTH DIMENSION

In the fifth dimension space and time do not exist but a particular vibration does. There is no space between things. How do objects exist without space? How do people exist without separation between them? In the fifth dimension you can be with another or at a place or event by THINKING about them. Dimensions are the DISTANCE from one **point of perception** to another point of perception. Our creator powers have been increased and we are fully in charge of creating our own PERSONAL REALITY and our own point of perception in every moment. When you do not like what you created it is your **RESPONSIBILITY** to change it. By getting in the cosmic flow with your entourage or soul you create the highest and the best for you and YOUR heart and then radiate that outward into your environment. That is the highest use to your human divinity.

The 5th dimensional beings include ascended humans and faeries our pets, other animals and the plant kingdom will also reside on this planet in their fifth density state. They will experience both the fifth dimension and fourth dimension simultaneously. They will be the teachers of the fourth density humans even though they are vibrating at fifth density.

The divine human commits to BE THERE when they are called to help with spiritual wisdom. Fifth dimensional humans avoid being evangelical and they reach out and touch another that ASKS to be touched and is not always verbally. Touch only those READY to accept your touch. The behavior that emulates the universal flow and oneness is to go WITHIN for YOUR answers and reassurance. For those you disagree with, oppose, fear or dislike, take the time and energy to educate you as to their beliefs and customs. FIND and focus on your **points of CONNECTION** and drop your focus on areas of disagreement. There is NO right or wrong in oneness AND when we are INSIDE ourselves. Become fully aware of the ***vibrational pattern you send*** out so you can understand what you get back and why.

Once we cross the invisible bridge to the fifth dimension life becomes simpler than the third dimension. Because it is a less dense form and shape, fifth dimension is SUBTLER and more ***graceful,*** light travels faster within it and our sense of time is very accelerated. To handle the stress of the acceleration we need be healthy.

The architecture in the fifth dimension does not depend upon WOOD, **steel** or CONCRETE. Glass is less brittle and more resilient because it is made differently. The fifth dimension has an increased sense of wellbeing for the individual and the community. The fifth dimension is not somewhere else, it is right here. We are in the fifth dimension if we think we are. The fifth dimension is a **spiritual shift** not a PHYSICAL move what you see is what you EXPECT to see. Our point of perception determines our reality. Every morning we wake up in the fifth dimension and a heightened state of creation and vibration and then we force ourselves back to the third dimension through our beliefs and behaviors. With higher vibrating crystalline light coming to earth you can experience the fifth dimension as a bright light being turned on in the form of gardens and intense loving light. Use the bright light to see with and increase your awareness.

Those that have shed their biology can move to the fifth dimension or the Garden of Eden, a fifth-dimensional paradise with beautiful, multidimensional light not seen on earth. You feel one with the energy of the garden. With all the changes and different energies coming and staying on earth we are being put in the position of needing to choose how we want to handle them. Do you want to fight changing from what has been and you are familiar with? Things will never go back to the old ways. Can you flow with the changes that will ultimately totally change you? Can you open your heart and mind a go with the flow. The change will be from using your thought or emotion to using your intuition or knowingness from your invisible parts your 90%er. No one can ignore the call to awaken. You must either grow and ascend in consciousness, or sink deeper into chaos, fear and limitation.

SUN or PORTAL

The sun is a DIMENSIONAL PORTAL for ENERGY and has been that way from the beginning of time. The sun is not an individual object. The warmth and gamma rays that enable us to live on earth come through from our sun portal. Our ENERGY distribution system is our sun. Earth and sun have formed a connection point or portal because they occasionally connect and stretch out through time and space. During those times of connection **particles are passed** from one to the other. We know those as solar storms. However it is much more than that it is the **life force** or sexual energy of the universe. The solar particles will carry anything you create.

The *heliosphere* OR the space around the sun which is approximately100 astronomical units in radius OR the **MAGNETICS of the sun** is at the lowest point it has ever been just like the magnetic grid is. The magnetics of this planet are linked to the changing consciousness of the human. Magnetics and universal love goes way beyond human love and are the same thing. A magnetic field that comes in contact with another magnetic field has the OPTION of transmitting its frequencies and patterning onto it. The SOLAR sun talks to our DNA by transmitting its energy and patterning into the magnetic field of earth. Our sun is communicating to you by sending its light in the form of a magnetic field.

The magnetic grid and the heliosphere have weakened and become more finite. The reason is that the magnetics are being finely tuned to speak to our DNA. With light or crystalline energy being spread on earth we all can SEE the dark and discover what we need to discover. Humans react to variations of light and not to light itself. We create our magnetic field and things magically show up and currently we are creating a new infrastructure for ourselves. All energy is infinite. The **magnetics** of this planet are linked to the changing consciousness of the human.

Earth is not sick she is pregnant and about to give birth to our higher vibrating thoughts. ANY entities, businesses, religions or groups that cannot adapt to the higher vibrations will fall apart or leave very quickly.

The new society we are establishing will have CUSTOMS instead of LAWS. Customs where each person is STRONGLY encouraged to carry their own **weight** and RESPONSIBILITY instead of playing follow the leader. We will not worship anybody else because in worshiping we give our self and our power away. We will discover how to create peace in our life and eliminate the drama and deception. Every step you take in integrity goes into the very core of the planet and into the grids.

Historically the only way to generate enough compassion on earth for a major shift to happen was to have a disaster. For the FIRST time human consciousness has raised to a place where nothing would happen no challenge of disaster or DEATH. A consciousness shift happened and we are having some changes without challenge. Coming to a third-dimensional planet does have limitations in consciousness.

STARGATES, VORTEXES, or portals are *energy fields* within, above and through the earth. They connect to the universe so ENERGY can be transferred through them. Stargates, vortexes or portals were present before the pyramids and the pyramids were built to keep everybody else out of the connection to the universe. Pyramid connections allow magic to happen. This energy can be used many ways.

HUMANS consciousness has been raised enough for the stargates to **open for communication** with other constellations and intelligence's, and other forms of life. There is now an expansion that the

Your Entourage is Waiting for you to find them

collective consciousness has agreed to experience. With stargates opening comes a trickle now and a flood later on of information and remembrance of where we have been and who we are.

The Arcturian STARGATE vibrates at a certain energy frequency. STARGATES can be entered when you match their vibration. Completing your ascension activates makes your frequency higher and through grace the ascension helps you to achieve this vibrational frequency necessary for the stargate. Part of the energy of the stargate must be in harmony with the planet from which you are coming. Many forces affect the stargate there is the Central Sun, ascension and the energy field of the stargate itself. Stargates, vortexes or portals are mainly, a conduit's of light facilitating transition for many higher beings from earth and to earth.

JACOB'S LADDER is a sacred conduit a corridor that is like a ladder and Jacob's ladder can lead to the Arcturian Stargate and fifth dimension energy. Connections to corridors allow higher beings from the fifth dimension to appear on earth. This happened to Elijah, he saw fifth dimensional chariots. When the corridor of ascension is open there is up and down movement. The third dimension illusions or matrix will no longer be powerful enough to cover the truth. Holiness is not only on the fifth dimension. You can create spaces in the third dimension that are holy and sacred. A sacred place can become a conduit to download greater fifth dimensional energy and light. Take advantage of this alignment of the earth with the stargate and ascension and new freedoms to chose and participate in your future incarnation process. You are able to travel instantaneously with thought and are instantaneously in the garden at the stargate. This is ascension and what is next

When the thoughts coming to you are inspiring and compassionate you are tapping into the wisdom of your invisible aspects. Spiritual enlightenment is not about following any guru or channel but it is for you to seek and find through personal discernment, through your inner guidance. When your goal is to meld with your soul you become a **living field of COMPASSION**.

We are all interconnected with the luminous invisible strands into a huge weave similar to a cobweb. As **your particular** strand is STRENGTHENED and healed by your awareness it is MOST important to YOU the individual and ESSENTIAL to the collective.

As you grow in awareness, the truth that was there all along comes to the surface, and it becomes easier for you to recognize it. **Know that you are worthy.** Awakening into a higher consciousness is often accompanied by feelings of urgency and strong desires to change. *Hearing and acting on soul communication is key.* When soul communicates with physical symptoms like aches and pains, sleep disturbances, headaches, lack of energy, feeling ungrounded or spacey and unexplained sensitivities to foods, LISTEN UP! Ask your biology what is most appropriate and DO IT. Releasing happens in LAYERS. Each dense layer or pocket of density, gone means more light can move into your biology. Patience, divine timing and a trust in the unseen world is needed now.

When we go into higher consciousness or fifth-dimensional consciousness our sense of time expands. We can slow time down by expanding our consciousness to experience the infinite. There are also ways of slowing time down in a pleasant way that helps you experience higher states of consciousness. Time is not an existing energy like space. Time has no mass or velocity.

Sacrifice is not even a concern because your point of perception becomes the souls point of perception. Giving something up that is VERY important to the little human causes an emotional reaction in the human the soul DOES NOT have. The soul IS NOT **attached to anything in this illusion.** So not having a thing, person or possession is not an issue for the soul. *The soul just changes focus.* The power of HUMAN focus means *greater peace of mind* and increased quality of life, especially in our relationships. When we allow our thoughts and attention on our self FIRST and then connect to one individual at a time so WE can FEEL and hear them *fully.* Then YOUR attentiveness and ability to communicate is far greater and AT A HIGHER level.

Small groups and one-on-one interaction is often more effective than larger gatherings because they are very personal and individual. **The power of one is about focus.** The habitual multitasker needs to change their ways in the new energy. Splitting your attention serves No one, especially NOT you.

When people succumb to coercion, force or control as in cults the lesson is in **accepting responsibility for your creation.** You know the truth but kept the truth hidden from your self. The duality of opposites on this plane has been a great teacher and growth cycle that has taken eons to complete. Democrats forget power comes from accepting responsibility. Republicans need to give financial resources to support people in learning to care for themselves. When support is given without the **acceptance of responsibility,** personal power gets destroyed. We support children and adults during a growth phase into a phase of taking responsibility for the self. *Progress IS NOT MADE when they are victims.* Are you not stronger for accepting responsibility for yourself?

Neither group, the ones getting a mortgage they can't afford. Or giving LOANS, mortgages to people that will never be able to return them. When you KNOW you cannot return money you take OR you know you are giving money you will never see again and the country at large will need to PAY the bills. There is victimization all around. Evaluate yourself realistically. Prepare for what IS and what you CAN manage. Be FULLY engaged in your experience. Evolve from being a pawn to OWNING what goes on in your experience.

Our THOUGHTS need clarity and integrity. An action taken secretively and with **guilt or shame** GREATLY affects your balance, calm and integrity. The exact same action taken while balanced and focused on the larger picture will have a totally different outcome. With the higher vibrations flooding the plant people who aren't interested in getting out of victimhood are welcome to stay there. The downside will be that being a victim or predator or silent witness will not be as easy or enjoyable as it has been historically. They will be MORE fearful, more **confused** and more INTENSELY emotional so CONFLICTS will increase around them.

Intensity of emotions is **not who** you are.

As the energies come in, those vibrating higher will absorb, align and release the energies through our biology rather quickly. You will experience the greater balance that comes from KNOWING who you truly are AND HOW YOU WORK. Watch and NOTICE when energy has *moved from the heart* into the solar plexus the survival and fear center. Is that the place you want it to stay? The heart integrates the masculine and feminine not the sex organs. The masculine energies coming in the end of 2008 will not be energies of control and force. The higher vibration of masculine energies is **stabilizing and protective**. Energy is just a TOOL and FUEL having many layers. Energy is created from nothingness. The nature of energy is to move in and out of definition. Energy in universal physics and goes back into itself and into a neutral state. **Nonphysical energy is electrical current** and at the basis of everything that exists.

Understand when people come to you for clarity and truth they are saying that yes, they want help or direction. When they keep coming they are deriving some benefit from working with you. When you say you won't see them anymore because they are not using your gift the way you intended YOU are THE ONE in the **middle of your own CONTROL issue**. You are saying, "You are not doing it my way, therefore you can't have my help."

THE TRUTH is they are coming because you offer them something. If you know there is someone who has the skills they need and you don't have, refer them OR work with them as long as they are respectful of your time and energy. Because things NOT happen according to YOUR agenda doesn't mean it isn't happening.

With every bit of compassion freely given a change takes place. Those that come are our teachers coming to remind us WE ARE LOVE just as they are. Accept them, **as they are**, WHERE they are. When you give **resentment** or *frustration*, they do not receive or FEEL the love. Teach by demonstration. That does not mean you do not set boundaries. When you get angry with someone else whether you know him or her personally or not it is because they are not doing what you think they should! That is YOUR issue and need for control.

A WALK-IN is the transfer of one soul leaving a human body with a new soul entering the biology. All have given permission for that to happen. There are billions of souls wanting or needing to come here at this time. Some for only a short time to create resolution of earlier experiences or to offer humans something and it needs to come from an **articulate adult** rather than a dependent child. Walk-ins occur mostly in adult situations. It is rare for a walk-in to take the place of a child.

Many of us came to earth in an ORB of LIGHT as the planet was being prepared for human habitation and many great beings of light are coming in an ORB of LIGHT now from far places to observers our shift. To avoid fragmenting themselves they travel in what could be called an ORB of LIGHT containing frequencies from which they came.

We vibrate higher when we stop JUDGING, stop gossiping, stop our NEGATIVITY and start loving ourselves. As we increase our LIGHT or awareness we have *increased power* and more RESPONSIBILITY to be COMPASSIONATE as your vibration raises your multidimensional qualities and awareness increase. Human fear and negative emotional energy is what the reptilian extraterrestrials feed on. So they have a lot invested in our lower vibrations and enjoyment of suffering. Reptilian's cannot totally dominate humans BECAUSE humans need to remain hypnotized and in deep unconsciousness for a prolonged indefinite period so we DO NOT notice how imprisoned we are. Humans if they were aware would be horrified to know they eat our children, drink our blood and prefer us to be in a deep state of fear when they drink and eat, as those are the chemicals that enable them to KEEP the prison humming.

Understanding the importance of the reptilians in our life and how they operate gives us choices. Know that they vibrate too low to feed off the higher energy vibrations. They keep and maintain the satanic cults around the world so they do not run out of their food supply. Through a variety of methods using our media, news and politicians they keep close to 80% of humans functioning like robots. Reptiles have no compassion or empathy for them selves, their children or anyone else. They want our energy and things to be predictable; they act just like the fuzzy monsters in the child's movie Monsters Inc.

    The main reptilian extraterrestrial families know who they are and bring up their off spring up to enter the "family business." The genetic code of reptilians lay dormant unless they are activated. Some of the bloodline family members are loving and compassionate without the lower vibrating aspects and some actively rebel against the manipulation and control that is ever present. Reptilian hybrids are looking for the encoded humans with skills they can use like politicians, banking, law and entertainment. Powerful people come into their lives and support them and "play" them until they switch the genetics from human to ACTIVATED reptilian. Rituals are used to open files or trigger programs.

Reptilians root for both sides in a dispute because the largest amount of rage and upset feeds them well. When you control both sides in any dispute you control the outcome. Control the democrats and the republicans you control politics. There will be no surprises. Reptilians want to know who wins the race before it happens.

The leaders live between dimensions and that space is without an energy source. The reptilians live in that space and feed off of human fear and negative energy. The reptilians in this space between dimensions BLOCK our CONNECTION to infinite consciousness.

Chapter 6
PHOTONS

Photons RESPOND ONLY to LOVE your THOUGHTS of love and photon to photon. Photons are the energy of LOVE and have different layers of energy in them and a particle of love. They are in a quantum state. As the reptilian LOVES low **dense, HEAVY** energies of fear photons ONLY FUNCTION with high vibrational thoughts and you will automatically draw photon energy to you and for you to use. Think loving, high vibrational thoughts and you will automatically draw photon energy to you and for you to use.

You can even breathe photons into your vehicle. Think and carry the photons down through your crown into your hands and through the nozzle to your gas tank. The first time you do this the vehicle might sputter a little in surprise, but breathe the photons on into your gas tank. You can breathe photons into your electrical appliances also. Each time you turn on a light or an appliance, breathe photons into the appliance. After the shift **PHOTON energy** will **REPLACE electricity.** We do not SEE the photon yet BUT it is present and working for you when you can control your thoughts to keep them positive like the cosmic flow. Be in love with who you are and what you are doing. Show gratitude and celebrate your successes. When you are not IN LOVE with yourself and loving YOURSELF you will be unable to access the photon energies. A photon is love energy of the universal type of love just like the energy that flows through your soul. Deep and expansive energy DETACHED and COMPASSIONATE love.

The minute one photon moves away, another takes its place. Using photon energy starts in your AWARENESS that is how you can work with it. The compassionate loving WILL of the human to use photons triggers their movement. Directing the photons, will accomplish tasks we want and need completed. This energy is VERY LIBERATING.

The left brain is the analytical side of the brain. The right brain is the **creative and holistic** side. We need to be centered in both sides to balance our energy. The photon is present all the time regardless of what you're thinking. Negative thinking will not diminish the photon, but it will not be AVAILABLE for your use when you think negative thoughts. All the photon knows and responds to is love. Photon energy TALKS to itself and springs into action based on the love it feels. When you amplify photon energy by getting it to talk to itself it gets stronger. The photon particles *talk to each other* in **present time ONLY.** The more love and photons you attract the better space you will be in. Photons will have increasing importance in our life.

    2012 is the marker for the time of "zero point energy" and the movement from MAGNETIC energy to CRYSTALLINE energy. During this time the earth will also be passing through the photon belt resulting in a symbolic "three days of darkness" and at that time the earth will embrace photon energy. This will happen quickly. The transition will be easier for those already working with photons. Earth is on the path to a SIMPLER more SPIRITUAL way of life. Your choices need to be made from that point of perception or you will be very frustrated. The photon energy is FREE and available now for the taking or using.

Photon particles are powerful energies that can **gather thoughts** and RETAIN MEMORY at a far greater rate than our BRAINS can do at this time. Photons know they are not a brain. The photon THINKS and is SELF DIRECTING in anyway that it is needed. Each particle of photon energy can **think and evolve** itself.

Imagine photons coming through your crown chakra and into your pineal gland and then into your thymus and the rest of your body. To heal others with photons put your hand on the healee's head and breathe the photon energy down through your pineal gland your thymus and your shoulder and out through your hand into the person's body or your own body. The body will feel it.

Our DNA emits photons with such regularity that researchers compare the phenomenon to an **"ultra-weak laser."** "A coherent source of light, like a laser, gives the sensation of very bright colors, or a luminescence, and the impression of having a holographic depth." DNA's highly coherent photon emission accounted for the luminescence of hallucinatory images, as well as their three-dimensional, or holographic, aspect. Photons vibrational ability can MANUFACTURE a **strand within the weave** of other energies to follow through and become a wavelength. Through the photon energy one can control EVERY **experiential** REALITY with the focus available in OUR matrix or illusion. Photons can control any energy field controlled by **electromagnetic force**.

You can practice supplementing your meals with photons bless your food and breathe photons into your food. The most significant aspect of the photon is the electrical arch or charge it has and its ability to relay messages throughout the body. Small electrical charges nourish and align the body to higher vibrations. Larger electrical charges run generators and things like that. There are charges to facilitate all types of activity. Charges to carry messages from cell to cell in the body. Photons are helping us rewire our body right now.

The photon cell can transfer energy from one end of the universe to the other end **without diminishing itself.** Photon energy can raise and expand levels of awareness in the human by SHIFTING their point of perception to a HIGHER perception. This would mean moving and expanding your awareness in any direction you allow or wanted to move into. Breathe pulling in the photons and start healing all of your four bodies, the spiritual, mental, emotional and physical. **First pull in photons from the spiritual realm** and then the MENTAL realm right through your thoughts, NOT the brain. Next, bring the photons into the **emotional realm, our HEART** energy located outside the biology, and finally into the biology. Your TRUST, **self love** and TRUTH need to be up and WORKING before you can take advantage of photon energy. Photons will be your life breath eventually. Our biology is about 70 percent water and WATER ENHANCES PHOTON energy.

With smog, pollution or smoky air, learn to breathe without breathing. Bring the photons in. Imagine the particles in through your crown chakra and then into the biology. As the photons in the air come in, you feel your lungs expand. Our thinking is creating our reality. If we want to get photons and not pollution, only take in photons. Communication will happen between you and the photon energy, and the photon will communicate with the one next to it and on and on. The photon is continually in communication one particle to the next. Hold your photons and use them for everything you want and then release them.

The photon energy is what you enter into when you get out of the third dimension and go in other multidimensional realms. Photon energy has started arriving on earth in larger amounts and is CHANGING OUR PERCEPTIONS by moving us into higher thoughts or AWARENESS. That is why awareness of satanic cults, government programming, sexual abuse, physical abuse and corruption are coming to light now. The Catholic Church and the Mormon Church and their controlling ways are being brought to conscious awareness by the higher vibrations that the photon energy brings. The publicity these abuses bring are helping define what abuse is and helping the public at large to give closer scrutiny to abusive behavior in our homes and institutions. For those functioning in the lower vibrations photons can be painful and very disruptive. Or when you are functioning on the fifth dimension and dip down into lower vibrational behavior it will hurt you.

Photon energy HURTS when you HOLD it.

When you are having a low vibrating thought and allow it to LOOP over and over in your mind, *remember a thought is a thing* IT GETS PAINFUL. You keep getting that spark of electricity EACH TIME you think that SAME thought over and over. The build up of those charges throws your body into an electrical storm, which unbalances you.

Having the higher vibration and the WILL to use photons accomplishes many tasks. This energy is FREE and available for the taking. The photon THINKS and is SELF DIRECTING in anyway it is needed. Each particle of photon energy can **think and evolve.** Apart from having energy a photon also carries momentum and has a polarization. Photons follow the laws of quantum mechanics, which means that often these properties do not have a well-defined value for a given photon. Rather, they are **defined as a probability** to measure a certain polarization, position, or momentum. FOR EXAMPLE although a photon can excite a single molecule, it is often impossible to predict beforehand *which* molecule will be excited. Photons carry of electromagnetic radiation and considered a MEDIATOR for **any type** of electromagnetic interactions, including magnetic fields and electrostatic repulsion between like charges.

VIKINGS

The Vikings interested me because they seemed to have followed SOME spiritual practices we are trying to get back to. Practices of equality the Catholic Church and other churches tried to quash.

Pre-Christian or pagans or Scandinavians or the Vikings had the rune alphabet from the first century AD until the 1300s. From around the 800s to around 1300s Christianity and paganism existed side-by-side borrowing from each other. Pre-Christian or Viking religion was an integral part of the society and the day-to-day life in all respects. Society always shifts and changes in its ways and customs. The early religions were set aside little by little because the Christians at that time would create wars with what they considered pagans and non-believers. The Vikings wanted to avoid bloodshed so they became Christians.

The Christian religion or the Catholic Church was and is a centralized MALE authoritarian religion was and is a power that did NOT ALLOW for individualized interpretation. The Christians wrote their religious beliefs down which brought consistent knowledge to all the Christian followers. So there was no flexibility. There was tight control on penalty of death.

Pagans used the oral tradition to spread their beliefs and traditions, which depended heavily on an individual's comprehension and memory so it was a very adaptable flexible religion for the individual and changing thoughts and awareness. Pagan religion allowed for individualized personal interpretation of their religion and had flexibility and equality for females which led religious activities that were carried on at home or in large groups in the center of town.

During Christianity women LOST their equal status and they became subordinate to males. Females in the community were associated with what was mortal and sinful.

Pagan religious power was based in their kin and home. When the Vikings treated their Gods well with sacrifice and then the God's favored their home. It was a working reciprocal friendly supportive relationship with the pagan God's. Christianity brought honoring a church building, the written word and the fear of not going to heaven after death. Going to heaven after death because you FAILED to follow the church or priest's rules.

The pagan religious followers had a good relationship with their God in life. Pagan's needed a good reputation in life and an honorable death going to heaven was not a consideration.

THE VIKINGS

The Vikings were farmers and sailors. They believed their world was fenced in and each god had their own private residences.

Thor—lived in the world of might.

Oden—lived in Valhalla the hall of slain warriors. After death the warriors fought on the other side with the gods against chaos.

Frejya—lives in the world of battlefields.

Frigg—lives in the marsh halls.

Baldr—lives in broad splendor.

Heimdall—lives in heavenly mountains.

PAGAN WORLD VIEW

Pagan's or Vikings believed in three worlds.

Yggdrasill—is the fenced in world and the axis of space and time.

Asgaror—is the tree growing at the center of the world and the treetop reaches the sky while the roots encompass all the world humans live in.

The third worlds the "other world"

Yggdrasill stands by a stream called Uror's well—The well decides human's fate and what time it is brought on. The god's protects the three worlds and those dominated by the enemies of the god's and man. There were three women of FATE that sat at the foot of the tree deciding human's future and fate.

DIFFERENT FEMALES

Three young **giant females** representing SEX, giant power and FRESH ACTIVITY invaded the world of the GODS. After the arrival of the three young females there is **creativity, fate, death and duality.** Man is created and time starts and a new world emerges from the cosmic sea. A new generation of gods rule and humans live happily. Religion or spiritualness was not a separate institution with special buildings and priests. Religion was part of ordinary life and was maintained by the individual members of the society. Rituals were performed in the homes of farmers and chieftains' alike. There were small rituals held at home and in major public rituals sacrifices were made to the gods to strengthen the Gods and the humans.

GIANTS—the world of the giants, they were huge, dangerous and coarse, wise and knowledgeable. The giants were the enemy of the gods and man. Giants and the gods represented duality in the worlds.

The world is born and ends in the battles between the giants and the gods. Aesir produced a superior culture. They were a creative culture and they lived a protected life.

Barr was a god who met and fell in love with **Bestla** a giant female; they were opposites and parented three sons. "Barr and Bestla" had **Odin** who was INTELLECT, **Vili** that represented WILL and **Ve** was sacred and they created the cosmos.

Before creation there was nothing but a huge void or space called chaos and the three sons of Barr the god and Bestla the giant created order and ideal conditions for humans.

This story of creation is comparible to the Greek story of their golden age and the Jewish / Christian story of the Garden of Eden

SOME NUMEROLOGY

Numerology is an ENERGY system and is **interdimensional**. It is the way things work in the universe and we have been largely unaware of it. In our linear string of reality we cannot stop time. It keeps going on no matter what! We are unable to reverse time. In multidimensions and PRESENT TIME movement is in all directions and **is circular**. You can see every potential possible for you and your neighbor and every one on the planet all-together in one place with no timeline put upon any of them. To the untrained eye it looks like chaos.

Master Numbers are **TRIGGERS** to humans that appear in our reality to get us ready for what is coming next. Many things are happening rapidly with the shift being in progress.

The **year 2007** has been a numerological nine and the end of **potential**. Duality contains potential, when you meld with your soul your potential becomes your soul decisions.

The **year 2008** has been the year of GLOBAL awakening or awareness and in this process DARKNESS has been stirred up to the surface and exposed to the light for all to see. Now we are seeing them it seems our global problems got worse.

The **year 2009** is about global BALANCING and that is rather **explosive**. 2009 is an 11 and the repetition of new beginnings. The number 11 mirrors each other creating INFINITY. A blank state as our DNA strands are being put back together into loops giving us new reality without time and space. Weather will change the face of earth. 2009 will cut into our old beliefs followed by a sense of wellbeing and better ways to balance our self. 09/09/09 that will be taking place September ninth of this year. It is a landmark. It is simply an opportunity to celebrate light in a new way because the old ways are ending and that is one aspect of the completion.

The **year 2010** will have a strong desire to fill up **from the inside** out. A NEW full and complete consciousness will be birthed in ALL MATTER. Everyone will be filled with the same hunger for awakening and the light to fill them up **from the inside** out. The masses step out of their linear path.

Your Entourage is Waiting for you to find them

The **year 2011** is the master number eleven doubled eleven-eleven, 11/11/11, November 11, 2011 is when earth will fully open up toward the cosmos again. All dimensions will meld together again and linear time and space ceases and we will step into universal unconditional love and higher truths.

The **year 2012** is the year of activation stepping into and leaving behind everything that came before and re-awaken as a divine human. This will **blend earth with Avalon, Lemuria and many other dimensions**. 2012 is when divinity and infinity resurrect itself in a field of neutrality or zero point energy will be our NEW reality. Zero point energy is a state of detachment, a measurement of UNIVERSAL energy at REST in whatever form it is CURRENTLY taking. They are the full spectrum of **color, sound and light**. On a macrocosmic level, dimensions are nothing more than light breaking through a prism. The veil has been perceived incorrectly it is a shell of light, a misty light in which we think we are trapped but we are not.

The **year 2013** is 3+1+2 = 6. By then 6 will be as infinite as one. All numbers will be one. We are in new energy now which means unusual things can happen to energy. Time is an illusion. Know we are a **vibration and frequency** and we are in control again.

On August 17, **2007**, Earth entered what is called the harmonic gateway. The planet will be in the harmonic gateway until August 17, **2017**. The harmonic gateway is a zero point energy field. It is an optimum energy field for **transformation of consciousness** on all levels. It is the time for transition between the end of the old Mayan calendar and the beginning of what is called the 2013 galactic Mayan calendar. On December 21, **2007**, the great galactic wheels aligned, opening the cosmic planes to what is known as the 2012 galactic wave. You need not wait for 2012 to come as we are there the vibrations will only intensify between now and the Gregorian date of December 21, 2012

On August 17 of 1967. Vast amounts of cosmic particles and energy forms began to surge through the solar system and penetrate the fear grid that surrounded our planet for so many centuries. This harmonic wave marked a time of social upheaval with consciousness shifting to **civil rights**, WAR PROTEST and **flower power.**

Twenty years later, on August 17, 1987, the harmonic convergence occurred when the veils thinned between the worlds and humanity began a massive awakening. Your DNA was time coded to activate your galactic time codes that were stimulated by the energies of the harmonic convergence. Massive numbers of people began to clear out **fear vibrations** to raise the vibration of earth. At this time we widened the separation between good and evil or dark and light. There is **no going back** to the repetitive cycles of the past. Those windows are closing.

History will not REPEAT itself.

The great cycles of time have aligned with the galactic forces to bring change. HUMANS are the catalyst for change on earth **on every level.** On a core level molecular structure and the relationship to matter is being altered. Old thought forms are changing. Our fear and rigid, destructive perceptions are transitioning into love and compassion.

Parallel timelines are intersecting, and we will often experience being on more than one timeline simultaneously. This may leave you feeling temporarily disorientated. It is a time when being grounded is very important. An entirely new galactic time is emerging.

One is the singular "**I AM**" vibration. The number one represents *new beginnings* in numerological terms. **OM** vibration is the unity consciousness as expressed in the third dimension. Oneness is what we are returning to in the fifth dimension. One is infinite and contains all things and signals the beginning of a point of separation.

11:11 is the *trigger to our DNA to start reconnecting* the cut strands of DNA so the linear illusion of separation will be over ACTIVATING the shift from duality into oneness. Opening the **portal** or bridge to ascension and our doorway home has opened once again on this planet. Humanity has twenty years to pass through the eleven, eleven gates to oneness. The 11:11 activation runs from January 11,1992 to 2012. The two sets of two ones signify the first reality traveling THROUGH to the second multidimensional reality.

Duality was allowed so the **INFINITE** COULD study itself as a **finite human.** Polarity has enabled us to experience individuality and aloneness and receive energy imprints, which have been necessary to play out our illusion or conduct our research to increase our spiritual awareness.

11, Two number ones together create a master number that represents **enlightenment and illumination,** each one means *new beginnings*. It is the SIGN, NUMBER and VIBRATION of this age.

2 represent duality.

02-02-02 humans noticed the first shift of the NEW energy.

20 represents duality.

21 working with the trinity and working with your soul or going within.

22 is mastery of the third dimension.

The number three in numerology represents a *catalyst* providing the push for transformation of one energy into another energy and never changing its core self. Love is a catalyst.

03-03-03 the magnetic grids were fully in place moving to the next level

333 or 9 in the third dimension is moving into the final stage where all are three's and has not finished playing out yet. We played so long in the third dimension that it is entering a third stage or the third millennium. Steps have been taken that never had been taken before. Different choices have **opened** us into the UNKNOWN.

Our entire existence can be explained by dividing by threes, the triangular shape defining the third dimension. Three is the base number for CREATION as all things are based on the **TRIAD**. The trinity will have a deeper meaning as we move into our next phase of evolution.

Number four in numerological terms is an earth or grounding number and means STRUCTURALLY strong. The only thing we carry from one lifetime to another is our spiritual knowledge like the mantel of god. **04-04-04** all the portals were firmly in place on earth. The crystal energy has been filtering in through the sun portals via sun flares to be stored in the tectonic plates of earth now.

444 is the number of mastery and empowerment of the **SELF** a representation of the *fourth dimension seen from the third dimension*. Our relationship to everything is changing and this is representative of this movement.

Number five in numerological terms is the energy of CHANGE.

555 triple five is a trigger that our biology and DNA is ready to receive our codes for divinity. "555" being noticed on our clock faces to symbolize the fifth dimension and the threes are not yet finished. 05-05-05 was Cinco de Mayo also.

555 is the beginning of the fifth dimension. The fifth dimension was being created in the land of Atlantis and during that time humans chose to see **LACK**, *limitation* and CONTROL. The not so subtle expression of **slavery** and GREED came to the greatly "advanced" planet of free choice. That misdirection of energy has showed up many other times including now. We felt the need to decide who could use technology and who COULD NOT. There was enough for all if we acknowledged everyone was playing important parts and contributing to the whole. The effects of our misdirection's in Atlantis are here now unrelenting warning and challenging our movement forward into the fifth dimension. That is why the word was handed down from our soul that WE ALL move forward or no one does.

"Spiritual competition" is one of the most destructive ways to misdirect energy. For example do you believe seeing the numbers 555 means that you are more advanced than those seeing 11:11? Our biology needs different signals at different times so the number triggers will NOT appear in **LINEAR fashion** there are many *circles on circles* and then you will repeat cycles more than once. There is **no order of importance** so please do not attempt to apply human attributes and linear time to the workings of our sweet invisible realm. Make life choic-

Your Entourage is Waiting for you to find them

es without spiritual competition and judgment, DISCERNMENT is the only way to go. Find one small success that impresses YOU and build on it. Find one thing that you absolutely adore about yourself and build on that it, that will serve you well.

The number six is the most sacred number and represents communication, and the "pipeline" to the higher self and the soul. In numerology, six is also mastery.

06-06-06 is the perfect alignment of COMPLETION. You are being real and true with yourself and in perfect alignment to move to the next level. **666** or six, six, six, the human sign for the devil is humorous to the invisible realm because we doubled threes. Humans are a manifestation of God in finite form.

666 could be evil if you try to control others OR you FEAR YOURSELF and your evolution. Do you fear your awareness? You will go into fear because you fear the beast within you. Each 6 represents an important aspect of our body, mind and spirit. When these come into full alignment it signifies the end of an old cycle and the beginning of a new cycle.

07-07-07 is a reminder and acknowledgment to our wonderful self of the now moment and our alignment, balance and completion of a cycle and the start of a new cycle.

08-08-08 is at number 6 in numerology. 8-8-8 is considered lucky.

The nine-year *vibration* of 2007 represents completion. 2008, which is a one 2008=10=1 represents starting over and new beginnings. Every nine years this occurs. You have a nine and a one.

When numbers align like 9-9, 4-4, the alignments are also a type of wink or nod from your soul to you. Saying it is nice that you are recognizing alignments and the synchronicities in your life that we have lined up for you. That way you see that you are in alignment with yourself and following the path of your highest potentials.

12:12 is a trigger to our biology that we are emerging from one dimension into the next dimension "two sets of threes." The date **12/12/12**, we are not ALL going to ascend for it is happening now.

2012 is NOT the end of the world; it is the end of a cycle and the start of a new spiritual cycle. 2012 is a marker for the COMPLETION of our **age of darkness** and the start of greater access to the higher dimensions. 2012 is the starting point for WHOLENESS and new beginnings of integrity within higher dimensions. 2008 until 2012 some humans have already accessed and moved into higher dimensions. Most humans will choose to remain in the third dimension.

INTENT and WILL are far stronger than any astrological or numerical influences. Trinity dates are important but NOT more important than moments of free will, which can accelerate the geometric activation of crystalline frequency speeding up the synergy.

GREAT SHIFT 1987-1999 was the first part of the great shift starting with the Harmonic Convergence and including the galactic alignment. The grid group came in 1989 and left in 2002, to build a matrix to change our DNA. The magnetic field grid moved greatly transmitting information and energy and a new quantumization to our DNA. The moving of the grid voided the energy of Armageddon and crystalline energy moved in and the Soviet Union fell. The Crystalline Grid is an interdimensional present time grid.

2000 to 2012 the Great Shift is part of the quantumization of DNA. It allows for the spiritual shifting of our purpose while we are in biology.

2013 to 2025 adjustment of human thinking and thought a shift to a higher vibration.

SPIRITUAL CONTRACTS or spiritual vows haven't been written since 1997 they are obsolete in the new energy. They were too complicated and exhausting for the invisible realm to manage and make work. They are pointless in the new energy. So if

Your Entourage is Waiting for you to find them

you want to release yours I would recommend you talk to your entourage about it at length.

※

ERAS, periods or CYCLES or chances to get it RIGHT one more time. During the "star wars" period the council and the order of the arch were fine-tuning the experiments they wanted to conduct on earth. The council members pondered questions about the type of magnetics to use, how much isolation would be best, what aliens to allow access to the humans and things of that nature.

Yes, aliens and or the reptilians invaded and have increased our challenges around ten to twenty percent more than were originally planned.

About 100,000 years ago HUMANS got new layers of DNA from the Pleiadians. The seeded humans SUDDENLY started to act out the process of **duality** and the awareness of light and dark and good and bad and them and us. The extra layers were ALSO a set up for the test or game of earth to become the *only planet of free choice* at this time. One layer would include the Akashic Record, which is the record of all the angelic souls who would come and go within the Human biology.

Humanity began to be spiritual **very slowly**, slowly over another 50,000 years. Angels began coming into the planet using the human biology as the vehicle to create the TEST or game of "the earth illusion" they played. Truly enlightened humans are only about 50,000 years old very new.

Approximately 40,000 years ago the age of **LEMURIA** was **80% light** and 20% dark. The Lemurians were very connected to their entourage and soul. Lemurian civilization existed in an elemental form, very primary or basic, for more than 5,000 years. Not huge in numbers but they were **HUGE in consciousness**. Lemurian civilization lasted more than 20,000 years in PEACE.

The Lemurians had a full-fledged mature civilization from 35,000 years ago to about 15,000 years ago. Remember things lasted a very long time and moved VERY SLOWLY in the early days.

AWARENESS and time moved lock step together. What takes us a year to accomplish today may have taken the Lemurians hundreds of years to accomplish back back in those days. Language and communication was new because they had functioned nicely with mental telepathy before they needed to use cumbersome words.

Then there was **ATLANTIS—40% light** and 60% dark. Atlantis lasted around four thousand years approximately 15,000 to 11,000 B.C. Control and manipulation was the order of the day. There is **old** Atlantis and **young** Atlantis, America. They are very far apart PHYSICALLY and in TIME. Old Atlantis was in the Pacific a settlement of Lemuria, which did not hold the Lemurian consciousness for long. Atlantis had a high vibrational awareness but it was not higher than NOW. It became the model for SLAVERY and **decadence** along with *misused technology* and the result of the evolution of HUMANS from Western Europe. This small group wanted to separate the soul or our entourage FROM the HUMAN and that became a VERY large group during Atlantis.

Some Lemurians ancestors today are the Polynesians.

One of the groups of Lemurians was called **Summerian** in the Middle East, eventually leading to the **Egyptian** civilization many years later 3150BC and ends in 30BC with the Roman Conquest.

There was the **CHRISTOS—20% light** and 80% dark remember the dark ages, not pretty. That has ended as we leave duality with our spiritual awareness increased? There are some stragglers clinging to duality

Now is the age as of 1987 of **RECONNECTION** with our 90% invisible parts. The human is moving into ones and melding with their entourage and soul again to feel and experience what our souls feel and experience peace, calm and JOY. The human has gone through different eras or chances to get it right on earth and a NEW era has started right now. We are evolving into a quantum leap in our spiritual awareness or remembering what we have always known and not accessed.

Your Entourage is Waiting for you to find them

CONTROL or FREEDOM

TO gain control of another, keep the human undisciplined and ignorant of universal laws and the way of multidimensions. Keep them IGNORANT, **confused** and distracted with matters of no importance.

The control the reptilians have over humans is the same kind of control our parents and culture have over us. The reptilians our family and culture control us be keeping us IGNORANT, **confused** and distracted. Look for the over all pattern to understand what I am saying. IT IS NEVER one incident that creates anything. It is a bunch of incidents that move you in a direction. Someone calling you stupid once probable affects you little. Someone or many people or events "pointing out you are stupid have the impact one you of making you feel insecure, you doubt and become fearful.

Reptilians and generations in the same family tradition create LONG TERM plans and behaviors lasting many life times. When you view a long chain of similar events you can know it is not just one event or one time you are seeing. It is always a long chain of similar events that create what you are and what situation you are in TODAY and right now. There was NO magic involved. What **magnetic energy** about how you THINK and feel about yourself do you what to emanate?

We have been controlled and fearful for so long we are afraid of our OWN light and power which makes our controllers the reptilians our family and culture VERY HAPPY. When you ALLOW your controllers to be responsible for you and your thoughts and self worth they are most happy.

Freedom from your controllers is a THOUGHT away. Your **thought patterns** of unworthiness and FEAR create your prison. YOU are your own prison guard. To open the prison door **control your thoughts** and take RESPONSIBILITY for who and what YOU ARE. Stand in your truth!

Esoteric knowledge, spiritual awareness and Mystic Knowing are neutral Knowledge just as universal laws are. Which direction do you want to take the knowledge?

Bonnie Baumgartner
Books and comments

My books are not LIGHT entertainment or is the information in them FUN. Humans by nature do not LIKE change. I am talking about subjects MOST humans avoid talking or reading about seriously.

When humans speak of there **"spiritual belief's** or their **dysfunctional relationships** with other humans they are hoping THOSE THINGS or OTHER humans will CHANGE so they can be more comfortable and not have to change them selves.

MY books will make you UNCOMFORTABLE.

I am asking YOU to change your **THOUGHTS**.

New thoughts mean changed beliefs.

Change your beliefs and you **BEHAVE differently** meaning those that like you the way you are will be unhappy with your changes.

My work is inspired and not channeled I am using my mind and my experiences.
I want a nicer, friendlier place to live in with MUCH less drama.

1. Healing Self-Defeating, "Nutty" Behavior

Is about the way to create a dysfunctional human child by not treating the child with love and compassion. To have a happy person you need to have treated the child well and loved it. Buying a child THINGS and telling them they are stupid is not loving. In this book I have shared what I learned teaching and doing therapy with the emotionally crushed spirit of the child and adult.

Own how CRUEL you have been to yourself.

2. It's All about Loving Yourself

Your existence is just that, it is YOUR REALITY and your reality is all about YOU. My reality is NOT your reality. My vibration and the things I PULL into MY life is probably NOT your vibration and what you have pulled into your life. We are all different, sharing the same planet. Have you noticed there are different bands of vibrations with different sorts of people in them? You know other humans in your vibration. You do NOT know the ones in different vibrations. That is universal law. In this book I also talk of how we got into the situation we are in, the history.

3. Love or Trauma: and Heal Multidimensionally

This book explains HOW to communicate with the invisible realm or your angels and guides. Your invisible entourage will give you more honesty and insight about you and your personal history than ANY group of humans are capable of doing. I want you to learn multidimensional THOUGHT and reality. To do that you need to communicate with your entourage. They know all the answers. They know which issue YOU need to address FIRST and how to address it. All you need to do is listen and DO!

4. Joyfully Being a 10%er

I was upset when I felt compelled to change my thoughts about what a grand human I was. To find out I was only 10% of something I could not see, feel or touch was VERY upsetting. To gracefully integrate that information took a lot longer than it took to write this book. Chapter 4 is about the sexual energy we need to deal with at this time.

5. KEEP IT SIMPLE

Living in the third, LOW VIBRATING, heavy and dense dimension has made us think COLLECTING objects and people are the way to go and be happy in 3D. Now we are moving on up to 5D and all that heavy stuff needs to go. YOU need to change your THOUGHTS about all that stuff's importance and RELEASE it. This book addresses how to work with different energies.

6. Ex p a N D i n g

So what does that mean? As our vibration as a planet gets higher and MORE SPIRITUAL that means **EVERYTHING is changing** and no one cares that you are not happy with change. Things are NEVER going to be like they were, so for your OWN mental health it would be good for you to put a positive spin on the changes or you could go a bit nuttier—Always your choice. I talk about our veil of forgetfulness in this book also.

In this book and every book after it I have added a dictionary of multidimensional terms and definitions. Associated with the "New Energy" are a lot of new and remarkable concepts. With new concepts will come new word definitions and dialog?

7. DIMENSION SURFING

Your soul at play is your divine intelligence. We are souls pretending to be humans playing the game of free choice. I talk about our brain, mind control, and brain overload, the chaos theory, quantum physics and reality and dimensions and time. Staying in the NOW moment we can move to acceptance and embracing that We Are God Also.

8. THERAPY with your ENTOURAGE

ENTOURAGE is a group of entities, not always invisible, attending to or surrounding the important human. Your entourage has entities coming and going all the time depending on the human's current need and choices. I write at length about the new soul groups of children coming on to the planet to help adults SEE more clearly what is TRUE we are multidimensional.

9. A SPIRITUAL SHIFT

The fifth dimension and its higher vibration, different truths, values and spiritual awareness is a hologram being placed over the third dimension causing the changes going on currently. This is not a physical thing nothing will "look different." What you see is what you expect to see. We are changing from the inside out and nothing is ever going back to the way it was.

10. JOYFUL EXPANSION

If you are waiting for someone to DO it for you or on your behalf you have a long wait. That is not going to happen in this lifetime. We have been invited by our soul and the legion of light to take a very active part in our life. We have been invited to ENJOY life at all times no matter what we do. You take your soul's hand and it will lead you.

11. FEEL GOOD

When you work with your entourage or soul, life becomes a great deal smoother because the invisible realm helps you see the larger picture and a different point of perception. I talk about their belief that a lie is generally an **aspect of the truth** that doesn't want to **OWN ITSELF.** That abundance is when you open your heart and realize that everything is COMPLETE in the now MOMENT.

12. THOUGHT SOUP

Is what we have lived in all the time. Now it is time to seriously discern which of the thoughts YOU care to swallow and hold. I talk of the auric mental body, the spiritual body and our emotional body and what we can find in the different bodies and how we can clear and heal them. I also take of our soul contracts and how they have changed since 1987.

13. FEELING is NOT OWNING

Is a large concept we need to embrace to increase our personal peace? Just because you thought it or felt something you do not need to take ownership of it. Our awareness of what goes on around us and IN other people is increasing with the higher vibrations. We know more about others than we ever have before and we tend to feel personally responsible when we are NOT. It is not about us, it belongs to someone else.

14. Remembering WHY

Why we are living on earth and reestablishing communication with our 90%er or our soul. This book talks of our inner space and inner channeling and reclaiming our aspects. How denial and compromise work against your communication with the invisible realm.

15. SPIRITUALITY

Is a joyful lifestyle, being guided by your entourage or soul and your heart takes all the pressure off the human. The invisible realm sets up all the synchronicities and probabilities. All of our relationships are changing; they are becoming more heart centered and compassionate. Deeper communication and UNDERSTANDING are happening at this time, so sit back and enjoy.

16. Levels of COMPASSION

This is a special book. The invisible realm loves things orderly and easily measured and everything in its place. There is an emotional level or vibrational scale for humans based on the level they function at most of the time. The level dictates your perception of reality, your TRUTH'S and BEHAVIOR and your SPIRITUAL AWARENESS.

For the first time EVER humans now have a scale for the divine human or ascension or soul melding. Instead of your guides and angels being in your auric field your soul resides there when you choose that and raise your vibration level high enough for that to happen.

17. SEXUAL ENERGY, Awareness Heals Me

This book is about understanding EXTREME abuse and control and how to break into and crash cult ritual abuse and government programming or an abusive childhood with YOUR awareness. The reconstruction process is also explained. Sexual energy is self-love. UNBALANCED sexual energy is abuse and control.

18. ENERGY WARS, Dense Dark or Expansive Light

The choice is **sluggish**, DENSE, **CONTROLLING,** dark energy OR **AWARENESS**, EXPANSIVE light energy dominating? The choice is up to each individual human to make. Ready or not humans are all going to be functioning in the higher vibration of the fifth dimension or going back to their maker.

Awareness is your **shield** in this war of dark and light energy

19. MULTIDIMENSIONAL DICTIONARY, Definitions and Concepts are in Process

Our world is SMALL, LINEAR and SIMPLE. Become a ***multidimensional thinker*** and expand your mind by including a much larger point of perception of our world. Awaken to your SPIRITUAL awareness, then your potential to THINK will really soar. Many of the definitions in my books are multidimensional CONCEPTS or feelings we do not have words for in the third dimension.

20. WINDOWS are CLOSING, Choices are Increasing

The windows of choice are closing faster than ever before. Our choices are a reflection of our consciousness that is also speeding up. When the invisible realm has aligned synchronicities on your behalf the length of time that option is available is growing shorter. We need to awaken spiritually by going within to establish and keep the lines of communication open with our guides, angels or soul. BEFORE you can lay a new realty over the illusion we are in you MUST **own and feel** all your experiences to heal them. That is the way of it. A human can refuse to listen to their voice within in favor of the little human voice. BUT it does become increasingly difficult to ignore the DNA activation code of ascension.

21. PSYCHOLOGY in the NEW ENERGY, LOVE YOURSELF FIRST

The **new psychology** is about the individual working with their entourage or soul in multidimensions to evolve and OWN their SPIRITUAL wisdom with honesty and integrity.

One of the rules of the game of free will is that your entourage can only answer the questions the human ASKS. The invisible realm always stands ready to help the little human or 10%er when they ASK for help and awareness. The human needs to ASK and **listen** within themselves for answers they seek. Your entourage knows your complete personal history in DETAIL. The invisible realm knows your conscious and **unconscious feelings** and understands what elements created the feelings you have or are not in touch with that you have. The invisible realm **NEVER judges or blames** the human. They have only compassion and information and support for us.

22. Your ENTOURAGE is WAITING for you to find them,

NOTHING is written in STONE, All is Change and Evolution. Book 22 the last in the series Mystic Knowing. The purpose of earth and the surrounding celestial bodies is to UNFOLD and EVOLVE life balancing and partnering with your soul. This requires your THOUGHT first followed with YOUR action and taking the **responsibility of sustaining yourself**, by nurturing YOUR joy and YOUR well-being.

Always be aware that we are eternal moving and evolving whether you pay attention or not. Life is the experience, and discovery of THE SELF. Joy of life requires ATTENTION and **focus.**

Made in the USA